OF THE NATURE AND QUALIFICATION
OF RELIGION IN REFERENCE
TO CIVIL SOCIETY

NATURAL LAW AND
ENLIGHTENMENT CLASSICS

Knud Haakonssen
General Editor

Samuel Pufendorf

NATURAL LAW AND
ENLIGHTENMENT CLASSICS

Of the Nature and Qualification of Religion in Reference to Civil Society

Samuel Pufendorf

Translated by Jodocus Crull

Edited and with an Introduction by
Simone Zurbuchen

The Works of Samuel Pufendorf

LIBERTY FUND

Indianapolis

© 2002 Liberty Fund, Inc.

Frontispiece portrait of Samuel Pufendorf is to be found at the University of Lund, Sweden, and is based on a photoreproduction by Leopoldo Iorizzo.

06   05   04   03   02   C   5   4   3   2   1
06   05   04   03   02   P   5   4   3   2   1

Library of Congress Cataloging-in-Publication Data
Pufendorf, Samuel, Freiherr von, 1632–1694.
[De habitu religionis Christianae ad vitam civilem. English]
Of the nature and qualification of religion in reference to civil society / Samuel von Pufendorf ; translated by J. Crull ; edited and with an introduction by Simone Zurbuchen.
p.   cm. — (The Works of Samuel von Pufendorf)
(Natural law and enlightenment classics)
Includes bibliographical references (p.   ) and index.
ISBN 0-86597-370-9 (hc : alk. paper) — ISBN 0-86597-371-7 (pb)
1. Church and state—Early works to 1800.   I. Crull, J. (Jodocus), d. 1713?
II. Zurbuchen, Simone.   III. Title.   IV. Series.
BV629.P8413   2002
322'.1—dc21   2002022575

LIBERTY FUND, INC.
8335 Allison Pointe Trail, Suite 300
Indianapolis, Indiana 46250-1684

CONTENTS

INTRODUCTION

John Locke's *Letter Concerning Toleration,* originally published in Latin in 1689, is widely known as a founding text in the history of toleration. It is usually claimed that Locke was among the first who defended a "modern" concept of toleration. This interpretation rests on the basic distinction between a "traditional" and a "modern" doctrine of toleration. The former sees toleration as a grant or privilege bestowed on individuals or groups by the ruler. Toleration is conceived not as a good in itself but rather as a temporary means to overcome religious dissent. The ultimate goal remains the reunification of different religions or religious denominations. The "modern" doctrine of toleration is marked by a shift to religious liberty or freedom of conscience. In this view, liberty is an entitlement that does not depend on an agency that grants privileges. The liberty-based approach to toleration amounts to a principled defense of religious dissent and implies the permanence and ineradicability of religious diversity.[1]

Although Locke's *Letter* marks an important step in the history of toleration, it is by no means unique.[2] It is part of a considerable body

---

1. For the distinction between a "traditional" and a "modern" doctrine of toleration, see Mario Turchetti, "Religious Concord and Political Tolerance in Sixteenth- and Seventeenth-Century France," *Sixteenth Century Journal* 21 (1991): 15–25. The distinction was taken up in the editorial introduction to *Difference and Dissent: Theories of Tolerance in Medieval and Early Modern Europe,* ed. Cary J. Nederman and John C. Laursen (Lanham, Md.: Rowman & Littlefield, 1996), 5–12.

2. For Locke's place in the history of toleration, see *Difference and Dissent* and *Beyond the Persecuting Society: Religious Toleration before the Enlightenment,* ed. John C. Laursen and Cary J. Nederman (Philadelphia: University of Pennsylvania Press, 1998), 1–10.

of literature on toleration that followed the revocation of the Edict of Nantes in 1685. By this measure the French king, Louis XIV, renounced the laws that granted toleration to the Huguenots—that is, the Calvinists—in France. It has to be considered as the last great effort of one of the European powers to bring about religious unity by means of force. It is thus no surprise that this act was met by an outcry of protestations in the European "Republic of Letters." The lead was taken by Protestant countries such as The Netherlands, England, Brandenburg-Prussia, and Switzerland, where the Huguenot exiles had taken up residence.[3]

II

Samuel Pufendorf's *De habitu religionis christianae ad vitam civilem* (Of the Nature of Religion in Relation to Civil Life, translated as *Of the Nature and Qualification of Religion in Reference to Civil Society*) of 1687 is one of the remarkable pieces in this literature. It is exceptional, because the doctrine of toleration is developed within the framework of modern natural law, a doctrine for which Pufendorf is well-known as one of the founding fathers. His main works are *De jure naturae et gentium* (*The Law of Nature and Nations,* 1672) and its abridgment, *De officio hominis et civis juxta legem naturalem* (On the Duty of Man and Citizen According to Natural Law, translated as *The Whole Duty of Man According to the Law of Nature,* 1673). The first English translation of *De habitu,* which is reproduced in this volume, was published in 1698. By then Pufendorf was already renowned in England and elsewhere in Europe. The last decade of the seventeenth century witnessed extended discussion of his work in learned journals as well as the first translations of his writings. The first English translation of *De officio* dates from 1691, the second from 1698. The French, English, German, and many

3. On the toleration debate in the French journals published in The Netherlands, see Jan Schillings, *Het tolerantiedebat in de franstalige geleerdentijdschriften uitgegeven in de Republiek der Verenigde Provinciën in de periode 1684–1753,* with a summary in English (Amsterdam: APA-Holland Universiteits Pers, 1997).

other translations of *De jure* and *De officio* that followed in the early eighteenth century testify to the lasting interest in Pufendorf's writings on natural law. In fact, they were to play a major role in the shaping of German, Scottish, and French moral and political philosophy up to the American and French Revolutions.

As Jodocus Crull mentions on the title page of his translation, Pufendorf's *Of the Nature and Qualification of Religion* may be read as an "appendix" to *The Whole Duty of Man.* In fact, it can be understood as an application of his natural law theory to the domain of religion and church. At the outset (secs. 2–5) Pufendorf argues that the state is not founded for the sake of religion, since religion is part of natural human freedom that cannot be delegated to the sovereign. The end of civil society consists exclusively in the security of the citizens, while religion has to be left to the care of the individual. For that reason, respect for religious freedom is one of the duties of the sovereign. Relying on the contractual theory of the state, Pufendorf denounces the revocation of the Edict of Nantes, arguing that the sovereign transgresses the limits of his power when he extends his rule to religion. If the ruler persecutes subjects because of their religion, it cannot be considered an act of legitimate rule but an unjust, hostile, or tyrannical act (sec. 6). In *Law of Nature* Pufendorf had also argued that the sovereign can be unjust to his subjects when he transgresses the limits of his power.[4] However, in that work he did not acknowledge a right to resistance but insisted that the people have to obey the ruler, even if he degenerates into a tyrant.[5] The new persecutions by the French monarch led Pufendorf to conclude in the present work that, when rulers transgress their bounds, the subjects have a right to defend their religion, even by the force of arms (sec. 52).

Important as it was, Pufendorf's fierce opposition to the French king should not be mistaken as a turn to political radicalism. While his advocacy of religious liberty amounts to a principled defense of toleration comparable to that of Locke's, Pufendorf's teaching proves more

---

4. *Law of Nature*, book 7, chap. 8, secs. 1–4.
5. *Law of Nature*, book 7, chap. 8, secs. 5–6.

complex when viewed from a broader perspective. More traditional aspects of his doctrine of toleration are brought to the fore when it is evaluated in the context of contemporary European politics, which he followed closely as adviser to some of the successful Protestant rulers.

III

Samuel Pufendorf was born in 1632 in a small village in Lutheran Saxony. Following studies in Leipzig and Jena, he took a position in 1658 as tutor to the family of Baron Peter Julius Coyet, the Swedish minister (ambassador) in Denmark. As a result of war between Sweden and Denmark, Pufendorf was put in prison, where he composed his first treatise on natural law, the *Elementa jurisprudentiae universalis* (*Elements of Universal Jurisprudence*, 1660). After a brief stay in Holland he was appointed professor of international law and philology (later natural and international law) in the Faculty of Philosophy at the University of Heidelberg. In 1664 he published his first important political work, *De statu imperii Germanici* (On the Constitution of the German Empire, translated as *The Present State of Germany*), under the pseudonym "Severinus de Monzambano." His controversial argument that the German empire was a kind of "irregular" state, because sovereignty was divided between the emperor and the estates, was widely rejected, and the work was banned in German universities and—because of its anti-Catholicism—condemned by the pope.

In 1670 Pufendorf became professor of natural and international law in the Faculty of Law at the University of Lund at the invitation of King Charles XI of Sweden. Here he published his major treatises on natural law as well as a number of supplementary and polemical essays. A brief recapture of Lund by the Danes in 1677 led him to move to Stockholm, where he served for more than ten years as privy councillor, secretary of state, and royal historian to Charles XI. In this function he composed two works on Swedish history and a comparative analysis of the interests and powers of European states, the *Introduction to the History of the Principal Kingdoms and States of Europe* (1682–86). With the publication of *Of the Nature and Qualification of Religion* in 1687,

Pufendorf recommended himself as adviser to the great elector of Brandenburg-Prussia, to whom he dedicated the work. In fact, he moved to Berlin in 1688 and served as court historian and privy and judicial councillor to Frederick William I and Frederick III, who was to become the first king of Prussia in 1701. Before his death in 1694, Pufendorf began writing the history of these two sovereigns, and he also composed a treatise on the reunification of Protestants in Europe, published posthumously in 1695, titled *Jus feciale divinum sive de consensu et dissensu protestantium* (The Law of Covenants, or on the Consensus and Dissensus among Protestants, translated as *The Divine Feudal Law: Or, Covenants with Mankind, Represented*).

IV

The Divine Feudal Law merits special attention with regard to Pufendorf's attitude toward religion and toleration, for it has to be seen as a complement to the present work. In his later work Pufendorf clarifies that toleration is just one means among others for dealing with religious dissent. It should be applied only when the reuniting of religions or denominations proves impossible.[6] In Pufendorf's view, the reuniting of Lutherans and Calvinists was possible on the basis of a theological system containing the fundamental articles necessary for salvation. In contrast, the differences between Protestants and Catholics could never be overcome, and the present text and its context in European politics explain this opinion of Pufendorf's.

As a consequence of the revocation of the Edict of Nantes in 1685, Europe was divided into two blocs: a Catholic bloc led by France and a Protestant alliance led by Brandenburg-Prussia. The latter was soon to be joined by England after William of Orange's accession to the throne in 1688. Protestant leaders such as Frederick William I of Brandenburg-Prussia perceived France as an enemy of Protestantism that aimed at establishing a universal monarchy in Europe. The divi-

---

6. *Divine Feudal Law*, secs. 3–4. Cf. the introduction to my edition of this work (Indianapolis, Ind.: Liberty Fund, 2002).

sion of European powers into two blocs was further complicated by the interconfessional structures of the German empire. The Peace of Westphalia (1648) provided a framework for peaceful coexistence of different religious denominations. It recognized the Catholic, Lutheran, and Calvinist confessions and guaranteed the rights of those communities established before 1624. Consequently, the line between Protestant and Catholic realms cut across the German empire.[7] In his early work on the constitution of the German empire, *The Present State of Germany*, Pufendorf had explained this confessional division as one of the weaknesses of the empire, describing in the last section, which he omitted in later editions, the attendant dangers. Among other things, he insisted that the German Catholic estates ought to be prevented from forming alliances with other Catholic powers against the empire.[8]

In the eyes of Protestant rulers, the danger of Catholic alliances was imminent after the revocation of the Edict of Nantes. This helps to explain why Pufendorf's analysis of the relation between religion and civil society is not confined to the question of "how far the Power of Sovereigns extends it self in Ecclesiastical Matters." This is the guiding question only of sections 1 to 7, where Pufendorf, as seen above, insists that the ruler has a duty to respect religious liberty. As the state is not founded for the sake of religion, the sovereign's power in ecclesiastical affairs is restricted to ensuring that "natural religion"—that is, that part of religion that does not depend on revelation but is accessible by the help of reason alone—is maintained and cultivated among the subjects (sec. 7). Like most of his contemporaries, including Locke, Pufendorf was convinced that the belief in God's existence and in His providence was a basic requirement of man as a moral agent. Being without this minimum of natural religion, atheists and blasphemers were deemed incapable of a moral life and excluded from toleration.

Pufendorf insists from the beginning of the work that, in addition,

7. See Joachim Whaley, "A Tolerant Society? Religious Toleration in the Holy Roman Empire, 1648–1806," in *Toleration in Enlightenment Europe*, ed. Ole Peter Grell and Roy Porter (Cambridge: Cambridge University Press, 2000), 175–95.

8. *The Present State of Germany*, chap. 8, secs. 4–5.

it must be examined "what bounds ought to be prescribed to the Priestly Order in Ecclesiastical Affairs." If either worldly sovereigns or churches transgress their bounds, this will lead to "great Abuses, Disturbances and Oppressions, both in Church and State" (sec. 1). Pufendorf's lengthy analyses of the origin and nature of the Jewish (secs. 8–9) and Christian (secs. 11–39) religions are clearly directed against the Roman Catholic Church, his central point being that according to Scripture no ecclesiastical sovereignty ought to be exercised by priests. Already in his *Historische und politische Beschreibung der geistlichen Monarchie des Stuhls zu Rom* (Historical and Political Description of the Spiritual Monarchy of Rome, 1679), he denounced the worldly ambition of the Catholic Church (the "Empire of the Pope" or the "Popish monarchy"). In section 35 of the present edition Pufendorf concludes that the religious controversies between the Protestants and the Catholics "are so deeply entangled with the Interest of the Popish Monarchy, that it is impossible for the *Roman Catholicks* to recede an Inch from the point of the controverted Articles, without diminution of their Authority, and endangering their great Revenues; so, that all hopes of an Union betwixt them and the *Protestants*, are in vain, unless the latter can resolve to submit themselves under the same Popish Yoak which they have shaken off so long ago."

Against Catholicism Pufendorf argues that the Christian Church has to be understood as a kind of college or private society, subject to the jurisdiction of the secular ruler. He observes that the original meaning of the word *ecclesia* implies not statehood but democratic governance. Elders or deputies who were instituted at certain times always depended on the common consent of the congregation. For that reason, becoming a member of the church does not change the function of any man as a subject to civil government (sec. 31).

The last sections of the work (secs. 40–54) deal with the question of whether the church "received any Alteration from its former Condition, after Princes, whole Kingdoms, and States did profess the Christian religion" (sec. 40). According to Pufendorf, there was alteration indeed. Whereas the early church had to be considered as nothing but a college or private society, the church is "now being put under the particular Protection of her Sovereigns" (sec. 41). By becoming Christians, sovereigns acquire peculiar rights in ecclesiastical affairs, because of the union of their duties as Christians and as worldly rulers. Pufendorf seems thus to acknowledge that, where a state-church exists, the relation between religion and civil society is not the same as before. This explains why in this section of the work he approaches the question of toleration from a different perspective. Toleration is now discussed in terms of "reason of state." Thus Pufendorf examines whether the sovereign's duty to preserve public peace and tranquillity requires him to promote religious unity in the state. He first affirms that "it is not absolutely necessary to maintain the Publick Tranquility, that all the Subjects in general should be of one Religion." However, he then adds, "It is to be wished, and ought to be endeavoured, to procure but one Faith and religion in a State." He further suggests that, "where there is not any Publick Form of Religion established in a Commonwealth, it is the Sovereign's care, that one may be composed." Whether a sovereign upholds religious unity in the state or tolerates religious dissent is a question of the "Common Interest of the Commonweal" (sec. 49). Depending on time and circumstances, sovereigns may either banish dissenters or "tolerate such of their Subjects as are of a different Opinion from the Established Religion" (sec. 50). Toleration is thus conceived as a privilege granted to dissenting individuals or groups by the ruler.

In view of the shift of argumentation in the last sections of the work, the question may be raised whether Pufendorf did not himself offer powerful arguments justifying Louis XIV's expulsion of the Huguenots from France. This is certainly not how Pufendorf saw it, for he goes on to argue that sovereigns are obligated to tolerate dissenters "if they, when they first submitted to the Government, had their Liberty of Conscience granted them by Contract; or have obtain'd it afterwards by certain Capitulations, any following Statutes, or by the fundamental Laws of the Land" (sec. 50). This applies to the Huguenots, who had been granted toleration by the Edict of Nantes. It applies also to the Lutheran, Calvinist, and Catholic communities in the German empire, whose rights were guaranteed by the Peace of Westphalia. Those communities of the officially recognized confessions that had settled after 1624, however, as well as other Protestant and Jewish communities without contractual guarantees, had no claim to toleration in principle. The relevant principle was, rather, that of *cuius regio, eius religio*, which Pufendorf confirmed in the last sections of his work, leaving authority in religious matters to princes and magistrates and making toleration an instrument to maintain political stability or to promote economic prosperity.

V

Except for the treatises on natural law, little is known about the translation and reception of Pufendorf's works in Great Britain. As the translations indicate,[9] his writings on religion and politics were met with considerable interest. While *Divine Feudal Law* was left to others, Crull, the translator of the present text, also had a part in disseminating the *Introduction to the History of the Principal Kingdoms and States of Europe*. It was first published in 1695 and reedited, at times amended, more than ten times by the middle of the eighteenth century. Crull's biography[10] may explain why he felt expert in translating the works of a German author into English. He was a native of Hamburg who applied himself to medicine, taking M.D. degrees at Leyden and Cambridge. In 1681 he became a member of the Royal Society but was unable to pay the fees because of lack of success in his profession. He subsisted principally by translating and compiling for booksellers. More telling than the few available biographical facts is, however, Crull's dedication of Pufendorf's work *Of the Nature and Qualification of Religion* to the right honorable William, Lord Craven.[11] Here he

---

9. *De habitu* had a second, anonymous translation: *Of the Relation between Church and State: Or, How far Christian and Civil Life affect each other.* . . . (London, 1719). The work includes a preface that gives some account of this book.

10. Crull's date of birth is unknown. He died probably in 1713.

11. William Craven (1606–97) is known for his long association with the "winter queen" of Bohemia, the English princess Elizabeth, who was the consort of Frederick V, the Elector Palatine. A Royalist during the English civil wars, Craven

recommends the work for sustaining a middle position between two extremes, one represented by those "who center the utmost Felicity of *Civil Society* in a Democratical form of Government," the other by "Mr. Hobbes's Monstrous Principles" concerning the unlimited power of the sovereign.[12] Hinting at the theory of sovereignty contained in *The Law of Nature* and *The Whole Duty of Man,* Crull first observes that according to Pufendorf sovereignty is not necessarily attributed to a monarch, but sometimes also to a council. Thus in theory Pufendorf accepts monarchy, aristocracy, and democracy as three legitimate forms of government.[13] Crull then points to Pufendorf's warning to young lawyers, contained in the "appendix" to the work, "to take care, that under the Pretence of maintaining the Prerogatives of Princes, they should not be prodigal of their Liberty and Property." For the modern reader as much as for Crull, the "appendix" is of special interest, because it is directed against Thomas Hobbes, whom Pufendorf calls "the first Inventer of this unlimited Power" [of the sovereign] and "the worst Interpreter that ever was in Divinity." This criticism was occasioned by Adrian Houtuyn's revival of Hobbes's opinion in *A Political Epitomy, Concerning the Power of Sovereigns in Ecclesiastical Affairs,* contained in his 1681 work *Politica contracta generalis.*[14] As the only modern com-

---

provided considerable financial support for both Charles I and Charles II. Later he was a member of James II's privy council and served as lieutenant general of the forces. After the Glorious Revolution, Craven concentrated on private activities. Among other things he is held to have been a patron of letters, because numerous works were dedicated to him.

12. Thomas Hobbes's (1588–1679) main work is *Leviathan, or the Matter, Form, and Power of a Commonwealth, Ecclesiastical and Civil* of 1651, in which he defends the absolute power of the sovereign.

13. *Law of Nature,* book 7, chaps. 2, 5. *Duty of Man,* book 2, chaps. 6, 8.

14. Adria[a]n Houtuyn (1645–1733) served as a lawyer at the Court of Holland at The Hague. Besides the *Politica contracta,* he also published works on the Monarchy of the Hebrews (*Monarchia Hebraeorum,* 1685) and on the Batavian Republic (*Reipublicae Batavae liber primus,* 1689). The only available study of his *Politica contracta generalis* (The Hague, 1681) is in H. E. Kossmann, *Politieke Theorie in Het Zeventiende-Eeuwse Nederland* (Amsterdam: N. V. Noord-Hollandsche Uitgevers Maatschappij, 1960).

mentator on the work has observed, in Houtuyn's theory "Leviathan has gone crazy," for the Dutch lawyer "defended a completely unlimited and for that reason also completely senseless absolutism."[15] Against this background Pufendorf exposed, once again, the limits of the sovereign power in ecclesiastical affairs. Thus he aims to demonstrate that, even when the subjects and the sovereign are of the same religion and when a church is established by law, the sovereign cannot claim the right "of being the Supream Head of the Church in the same sense, as he is the Supream Governour of the State." As the church and the state are established for different ends, the prerogatives of the prince are limited to those "external" aspects of religious worship that are independent of its "internal" part.

In the second place, Crull insists that Pufendorf did not entirely separate the Christian religion from the state. This seems of special importance to him, because in most Christian states of the time religion was linked to the civil government, whether they retained or abolished episcopacy. After the Glorious Revolution, toleration in England was meted out in terms of the relationship between the established church and various groups of Protestant Dissenters, and Crull seems to suggest that Pufendorf's teaching was well-suited to support the position of moderate, if not latitudinarian, churchmen.[16] Thus the translator concludes the dedication with an appeal to those among the English clergy who have lately excelled by "convincing such as differ from them in Opinion, rather by strength of Argument, than any forcible Means." It may well be that the more traditional aspects of Pufendorf's doctrine of toleration made it attractive to the moderates in England who wished to secure toleration of religious dissent without questioning the established church.

15. Kossmann, *Politieke Theorie*, 64.

16. We can only speculate whether Crull dedicated the present work to Royalists such as Craven for mere financial reasons or whether he hoped to win them over to the cause of moderation.

Note on the Text and Annotations

The text has not been modified. Obvious printer's errors have been silently corrected, but the text has had the benefit of any doubts. Most of the notes are the translator's reproduction of Pufendorf's references to the Bible; to these Crull has added his own references. In both cases, any mistakes made by either Crull or the typesetter have been silently corrected through comparison with Pufendorf's original Latin text and with the Bible. In some cases, Crull has entirely omitted Pufendorf's references; these have been added and are marked "Puf." The remaining notes are by the editor and have been marked "SZu."

OF THE
Nature and Qualification
OF
RELIGION,
In Reference to
Civil Society.

WRITTEN BY

Samuel Pufendorf,

Counsellor of State to the Late
King of *Sweden.*
Which may serve as an *Appendix*
to the Author's *Duty of Men.*
Translated from the Original.

LONDON.

Printed by *D. E.* for *A. Roper,* at the *Black Boy,*
and *A. Bosvile,* at the Dial, both over against
St. *Dunstan's* Church in *Fleet-street.* 1698.

Introductory Epistle,
Presented to the

WILLIAM,
Lord Craven,
Baron Craven

OF

HAMSTEAD MARSH.[1]

My LORD,
THE extraordinary Character you have acquir'd by the joint Consent of those that have the Honour of your Acquaintance, Encourages me to deviate from the common Road, used by our Modern Authors; being made sufficiently sensible, how much a Mind endow'd with Genorous and Modest Inclinations (the inseparable Companions of a Great Soul) disdains the fulsome Praises, which those Gentlemen make the Chief Subject of their Dedications, whenever they pretend to Court the Patronage of Persons of Quality, in behalf of their Treatises. I must confess, I should scarce have had so much Presumption thus to intrude my self into your Lordship's Favour, if I had not been sufficiently persuaded, that the Renown our Author has so deservedly gain'd both here and abroad (and that under the Protection of some of the greatest Princes in Europe*) would be prevailing enough with your Lordship, to pardon an Undertaking, which, if in it self justifiable in nothing else, might perhaps claim the benefit of a general Custom from your Goodness. The Reputation of our* Author *being so universally and unquestionably established among all such as have a true relish*

---

1. See note 11 to the editor's introduction. [SZu]

3

*of Learning, I might without the least Prejudice to him, supercede to en-
large here upon this Treatise, if it were not rather out of a desire to satisfie
the Curiosity of some, who believe to have sufficient Reason for certain
Objections made against some Assertions contained in this Treatise, than
with an Intention to make the least Addition to a Piece, which, whether
in regard of the nicety of the Subject it Treats of, or of the Concatination
and force of its Arguments, deserves to be reckoned among the best now
extant in* Europe.[2] *Those, who center the utmost Felicity of* Civil Society
in a Democratical form *of Government, have not been wanting to charge
our* Author *with too much Passion* for *that Doctrine,* of Passive Obedience, *which leaves Subjects to the absolute Disposal of their Princes; But,
besides that, the* Appendix *annexed to this* Treatise, *written by our* Author,
in opposition to Mr. Hobbes's *Monstrous Principles concerning this unlimited* Power,[3] *may sufficiently clear him from this Imputation; If these
Gentlemen would have taken the pains to make a due comparison of the
several Passages both in this, and other Treatises of our* Author,[4] *relating
to this Subject, they might, without much difficulty, have been convinc'd
of their Error; As far as I am capable of penetrating into the Matter, it is
the word* Princeps, *or* Prince, *which sticks most closely in their Stomachs,
not considering, That the Words,* Summi Imperantes, *or* Sovereigns; *and
that of* Princeps, *or* Prince, *are Synonyms to our* Author; *and that out of
a great many Passages in this* Treatise, *it is sufficiently apparent, that he
attributes the Sovereign Power not always to one single Person, but sometimes also to a Council invested with the Supream Administration of the
Sovereign Authority in the Commonwealth. If it were but only for that
Advice given by our* Author *at the very beginning of his* Appendix *to*

---

2. The translator refers here to Pufendorf's *The Whole Duty of Man.* See section
II of the editor's introduction. [SZu]

3. See note 12 to the editor's introduction. [SZu]

4. I.e., in *The Law of Nature* and in *The Whole Duty of Man.* Pufendorf's relation
to Hobbes is discussed in Fiammetta Palladini, *Samuel Pufendorf discepolo di Hobbes:
Per una reinterpretazione del giusnaturalismo moderno* (Bologna: Il Mulino, 1990);
and in Richard Tuck, *The Rights of War and Peace: Political Thought and the International Order from Grotius to Kant* (Oxford: Oxford University Press, 1999),
chap. 5. [SZu]

young Lawyers, to wit, *to take care,* that under the Pretence of maintaining the Prerogatives of Princes, they should not be prodigal of their Liberty and Property, *and his asserting the Foundation of* Civil Societies *to be built upon the* Common Consent *of mutual Defence against Violences; This alone, I say, might be a convincing Argument to any unbyass'd Person, that his Aim was very remote from maintaining an Arbitrary Power in the State. The next thing laid to our* Author's *Charge is, that he so entirely separates the Christian Religion from the State, as not to have the least Interference with one another; whereas the contrary is now a-days practised in most Christian States, and in the Commonwealth of the* Jews *(instituted by God's peculiar Direction) this Union was inseparable. It cannot be denied, but that the outward Form of Church Government, especially among the* Protestants, *is in a great measure, and in most places adapted to that of the* State; *it being evident, that most of the* Monarchical States, Episcopacy, *as most suitable with that Constitution, was never abolished; as on the contrary, the same was quite extirpated in the* Protestant Commonwealths. *This is most particularly observable among the* Lutherans, *who, tho' all agreeing in Point of Doctrine, are nevertheless, so far different from one another in the Ceremonial Point, and outward Form of Church Government, that in outward Appearance, they seem'd to be so many several Churches. Thus in the two Northern Kingdoms of* Sweden *and* Denmark, *the Episcopal Authority (tho' much diminished in its Revenues) is retained to this day; whereas in some Commonwealths in* Germany, *where the same Religion is Established, it is quite abolished, and not the least footsteps of Subordination of Priests to be met with. But this Objection is easily cleared, if we take into due Consideration, that is being the Intention of our Author to represent in those pieces Religion in its genuine and native Constitution, freed from all what is foreign to its true Genius, he did not think it convenient, to clog it with any thing that was not an Essential part of it; especially when his chief aim was to shew the real difference betwixt the Christian and Jewish Religion. There are also not a few, who prompted by a preposterous Zeal, have imputed to our Author a certain kind of* Libertinism *in Religion, for which, I can see no other Reason, than that they are dissatisfied with his Assertions against any thing that has the least resemblance of Persecution upon the score of Dif-*

ference of Opinions. I am well satisfied, that the Reasons alledged by him, are so solid in themselves, and so exactly applied to this Purpose, that they cannot but be Convincing to all such, as are not prepossessed either with By-Interest, or a most stupid Ignorance, For, if the Slavery of the Body be absolutely repugnant to the Inclinations of a generous Soul, How much more insupportable must the Slavery of the Mind be to a sublime Genius, elevated above the common Sphere of bigotted Zealots Ignorance, being the Mother of perverted Zeal, and consequently of a persecuting Spirit, the same ought to be look'd upon as the common Enemy of all such as are guided by the Light of true Reason? I cannot but take notice here, that our English *Modern Clergy has of late gain'd so peculiar a Character of following so closely these footsteps of convincing such as differ from them in Opinion, rather by strength of Argument, than any forcible Means, that I do not know whether they are not preferrable in this Point, before any other in* Europe. *If any one questions the Truth of it, I appeal to Mr.* Toland's *Case, concerning his Treatise, Entituled,* Christianity not Mysterious.[5] *It is both beyond my scope, and the compass of a Letter, to enter upon the Merits of the Cause on both Sides, it will be sufficient here to refer my self to what has been Published against him lately here in* England, *and in other Places; All which, if duely compared, will soon evince, how much the* English *Clergy has out-done the rest, both by force of Argument, and a generous, gentle Behaviour. But I am afraid I have abused your Lordship's Patience; I will therefore conclude with recommending both my* Author *and my Self, to your Lordship's Protection, begging Leave to subscribe my self,*

My Lord,

Your Devoted Servant.
J. Crull. M. D.

5. John Toland (1670–1722) was an Irish-born British freethinker. His *Christianity Not Mysterious,* published in 1696, caused a public uproar. A great many books and pamphlets were directed against the work. The Irish parliament condemned the book and ordered Toland's arrest. [SZu]

THE

CONTENTS

7

Of the Nature and Qualification of Religion, in Reference to Civil Society, &c.

ℒℴℒ

Among all those Questions, which have for many Ages past been Controverted among Christians, this may be deem'd one of the Chiefest; which Treats of the Nature, Authority, and Power of the Church; and which of the several Christian Sects ought most justly to claim the Title of the *True Church.* The *Romanists*[6] keep this for their last Reserve, when Engag'd with the *Protestants,* That they Attribute the Name of the *True Church* only to themselves, and boldly stigmatize all such as are not of their Communion, with the Names of rebellious Deserters. This is the main Bulwark they rely upon; thinking it sufficient to Alledge in their own behalf; That they are not obliged so strictly to Examin, and maintain every Article of their Faith against the *Protestants;* since, whatever Objections may be made out of the Holy Scripture, the same ought to be rejected as Erroneous, if not agreeable with the Interpretations and Traditions of their Church; Thus making themselves both Judges and Witnesses in their own Cause. Besides this, it is to be look'd upon as a Matter of the greatest Consequence, both in regard of the Christian Church, and the Publick Safety in a State, to know exactly, what bounds ought to be prescribed to the Priestly Order

6. The Latin reads, "Those who follow the sect of the Roman Pontiff." Pufendorf usually speaks of the "Roman Catholicks." He never uses the simple expression "Catholicks," because he rejects the idea that the Roman Catholic Church represents the "Catholic" church in the true sense of the word. See section 35, below. [SZu]

in Ecclesiastical Affairs; as likewise to determin, how far the Power of Sovereigns extends it self in Ecclesiastical Matters: For, if either of them transgress their Bounds, it must of necessity prove the Cause of great Abuses, Disturbances and Oppressions, both in Church and State. I was the sooner prevail'd upon to Search into the very bottom of this Question, at this juncture of Time, when not only the *Romish Priests* apply all their Cunning for the rooting out of the *Protestants,* but also some of the greatest Princes in Christendom (setting aside the Antient way of Converting People by Reason and force of Arguments) have now recourse to open Violence; and by Dragooning, force their miserable Subjects to a Religion, which always appear'd abominable to them. But if we propose to our selves to examin this Point, according to its own solid Principles (as we ought to do) without having recourse to Ambiguous Terms and Tergiversations, it is absolutely requisite, that we trace the very Original of Religion in General; and of the Christian Religion in Particular, so as to Examin both their Natural Qualifications in reference to Civil Society. For, if this, which is to be look'd upon as the Foundation Stone, be well Secured: And we afterwards do look into the Scriptures, to investigate, in what manner Christ himself has represented his Doctrine to us; it will be no difficult Task to judge, whether, according to the Institution of our Saviour, there ought to be an Ecclesiastical Sovereignty exercised by *Priests?* Or, whether Princes have a Right to make use of an Absolute Power? Or can Compel their Subjects to Obedience by Force of Arms, in Matters of Religion?

Concerning Religion before Civil Societies were Instituted.

§1. That there is a Supream Being, the Author and Creator both of the Universe, and especially of Mankind, which ought to be acknowledged and worshipped as such by Menkind, as they are Rational Creatures, has been generally receiv'd, not only among Christians, but also by most of the Pagan Philosophers, that to pretend to demonstrate it here, would be Superfluous, and perhaps might be taken as done in prejudice of the judicious Reader; since, scarce any body, that is not beyond his right Wits, can be supposed, now a days, to make the least Doubt of the Verity of this Assertion. The true Knowledge of Divine Worship arises from two several Springs: For, we either by true Ratiocination, deduced out of the Light of Nature, may be Convinced of those Sentiments we ought to have of God, and what Reverence is due to him from us Mortals: Or else, some Matters, being beyond our Apprehension, by the bare Light of Nature, are by God's special Command Revealed to Mankind. Both Kinds are to be the Subject of the following Treatise; with this Restriction nevertheless, not to insist upon each particular Head of either of them, any further, than they have relation to Civil Society.

§2. The first Thing which is to be considered, both in Natural and Revealed Religion, is, That every body is obliged to worship God in his own Person, Religious Duty being not to be performed by a Deputy, but by himself, in Person, who expects to reap the Benefit of religious Worship, promised by God Almighty. For Man, being a rational Creature, owing its Off-spring to God alone, is thereby put under such an indispensible Obligation, that the Consideration of worshipping him, to the utmost of his Power, can never be entirely extinguished in a rational Soul. And here lies the main difference betwixt that Care, which, we ought to have of our Souls, and that of our Bodies; the latter of which, may be committed to the Management of others, who being to be Accountable for all Injuries, which may befall us under their Tuition, we are thereby freed from any Guilt against our selves. So do we commit our selves, when we pass the Seas, to the Management of the Master of a Ship, by whose sole Care, without our own Assistance, we are conducted to the desired Port. But, no body can so entirely transfer the Care of his Soul, and the Exercise of Religious Worship from himself to another Man, as to make him alone Accountable for all Miscarriages, and to free himself from Punishment. *Every one of us shall give Account of himself to God.*[7] And it is in vain for St. *Paul* to wish, *to be Accursed from Christ, for his Brethren, his Kinsmen, according to the Flesh.*[8] And, though it is undeniable, That those who have been negligent in taking care of other Peoples Souls, that were

Every Man is accountable for his Religion.

7. Rom. 14:12.
8. Rom. 9:3.

committed to their Charge, shall receive Punishment; Nevertheless, these, whose Souls have been thus neglected, shall perish with them, for having put too much Trust in others, and neglected their own Salvation. As it is plainly expressed by the Prophet *Ezekiel,* 33:7, 8. *And the Just shall live by Faith.*[9] And the Evangelist St. *Mark,* speaks without any Reservation. *He that believed not, shall be damned;*[10] without distinction, whether you were seduced by others, or whether you have renounced your Faith for worldly Ends.

How the same is to be exercised in the free State of Nature.

§3. From whence it is evident, That, Religion having its relation to God, the same may be exercised without the Communion of a great many; And, that a Man ought not to judge of the Soundness of his Doctrine or Religion, by the Number of those that adhere to it. So, that it is manifest, That, at the beginning of the World, our first Parents might, and did really perform Religious Duties; And, that, if one alone, or a few together, live in a solitary Place, they are therefore not to be deem'd to live without Religion, because, they do not make up a Congregation. For, God being the only Judge, of what is best pleasing to him in his Worship, knows and searches the very bottom of our Hearts; And, since we are not able, without his Assistance, to perform religious Duties, the same can't be esteem'd properly our own Invention. As those that live in the free State of Nature, are not Subject to any Human Power, So, in the same State, their Religion, having only a relation to God Almighty, unto whom alone they are bound to pay Reverence, it is free from all Human Force or Power; which, in this State of Natural Freedom, they may exercise, either according to the Dictates of Reason, or, according to Divine Revelation; and, according to the best of their Knowledge, may dispose the outward Form of their religious Worship, without being accountable to any body, but God Almighty: Neither can they be Controuled, or forced, rather to worship God according to another's, than their own Opinion. But, if any body pretends to bring them over to his Side, he ought with suitable Arguments, to

9. Hab. 2:4.
10. Mark 16:16.

Convince them, how far he is in the Right, and they in the Wrong. There may be, besides this, another Reason be given, why no body, in what Condition soever, ought to be forced to another Man's Religion; because the Knowledge of Truth can't be implanted in us, without proper and convincing Arguments, such as are capable of preparing our Minds for the receiving of the True Doctrine of Religion: And, as to the Mysteries of the Christian Religion, which transcend our Reason, these must be acquired by the assistance of Divine Grace, which is contrary to all Violence. 'Tis true, a Prince may force a Subject to make an outward Confession by way of Mouth, to comply in his Behaviour, with his Commands, and to dissemble his Thoughts or to speak contrary to his Belief; but he can force no body to believe contrary to his own Opinion. For we ought *to believe with all our Hearts;*[11] but, whatever is done in order to obtain any worldly Advantage, or to avoid an imminent Evil of this kind, can't be done with all our Heart. But, *Faith cometh by Hearing, and Hearing by the Word of God.*[12] Neither does our Saviour force his Word upon us; but by all gentle means, persuades us to a Compliance with his Will, according to St. *Paul's* Saying: *Now then we are Ambassadors for Christ, as though God did beseech you by us, we pray you in Christs stead, be ye reconciled to God.*[13]

§4. It is an unquestionable Truth, and generally received among Mankind, That one is obliged to give a helping-hand to another in several Respects: In the same manner it is with Religion; that these who by nearest of Blood, are in Duty bound, to take Care of young Peoples Education, ought at the same time to Instruct them in the true Knowledge of God, and prepare their Minds for the receiving of the Christian Doctrine. 'Tis upon this score, that this Care touches most nearly all Parents, in regard of their Children, it being the principal Part of Paternal Duty, to take effectual Care, that they may be throughly Instructed in all Matters, relating to God and his holy Word; and to be

The first Care of religious Worship lodged in Parents.

11. Acts 8:37.
12. Rom. 10:17.
13. 2 Cor. 5:20.

encouraged in all manner of religious Exercises: For it is too dangerous, to leave young People to their own Inclinations, till they may be capable, by the Strength of their own Reason, to learn their Duty towards God. And it would be much more dangerous, to defer it under pretence or expectation of Revelations to be made upon that account, at this time, when the Word of God is already planted and established among us: Besides, that Children soon grow head-strong and refractory, if they are not in their tender Age, accustomed to pious Exercises. Nevertheless, Parents ought not to exercise this Paternal Office any otherwise, than in a manner suitable to the Genius of the Christian Religion, which will have them not to act with Violence, but to be diligent and assiduous in Teaching, Exhorting, Praying, and announcing God's Wrath. Wherefore, the Priestly Office was originally joined with the Paternal, in the antient Fathers of Families; and *Abraham* is commended both for a good Father, and a good Master of his House, because he instructed his Children in all manner of Piety, and himself Administred Circumcision.[14] The like Commands were made to Parents, both in the Old and New Testament;[15] and the Patriarch *Jacob,* removed the Idols out of his Family, not by Compulsion, but by Instructing those of his House in the Knowledge of the true God, who thereupon, voluntarily surrendered those Idols to his Disposal.[16] This part of the Paternal Office, like all the rest, does cease as soon as a Son, after leaving his Father's House, comes to set up for himself, and consequently becomes the Father of a separate Family, and enjoys the same Rights, which his Father had before over him. And, tho' perhaps in such a Case a Father may still retain the priviledge of giving some Paternal Admonitions to his Sons, yet ought the same to be look'd upon to resemble in their Nature our last Will or Testament, which does not always imply properly a Command; but ought to be observed for its good Intentions sake, and to shew a due Reverence to the Mem-

14. Gen. 18:19.
15. Deut. 6:7, 11:19; Eph. 6:4.
16. Gen. 35:2, 3, 4.

ory of a Father, never to be neglected by any, that will not at the same time profess themselves guilty of Improbity.

§5. Out of what has been said before, it is most evident, That Civil Governments were not erected for Religions sake; or that Men did not enter into Civil Societies, that they might with more conveniency establish, and exercise their Religion. For, since Religious Exercises could be performed as well by a few, as by a great Number; and in a small Congregation as well as in a great one, it was unnecessary to erect several great Societies on that account: Besides, that those who committed open violences against others, which was the first motive that obliged Men to enter into Societies for their mutual Defence, did not aim at the Religion of Mankind; but, to robb these that were weaker than themselves of their Liberty, Life, and Fortunes. Neither does a Man's Probity and Piety receive the least addition, by the Number of People, which join in their Devotion; For every one must be acceptable to God Almighty upon his own account; neither is a Man always deem'd the more pious, because he lives among such as are pious themselves. Those Patriarchs that liv'd before Civil Societies were erected, are no less Famous for their Piety, than those that lived afterwards under a settled Government. From whence it is evident, That Religion is not an ingenious Invention of the first Founders of Commonwealths, but as antient as Humane Race it self; it being sufficiently apparent, that Mankind did not enter into Civil Societies; till long after, being enforced thereunto, by great and weighty Reasons; tho' at the same time, it cannot be deny'd, but that some have cunningly abused Religion, for obtaining their Ends in the State; But, Religion in it self considered, Is not made subordinate to the State; or to be deem'd a proper Instrument to serve a States Turn, and to keep the People in Obedience. And, when Religion is called, *Vinculum Societatis Civilis, The Cement of Civil Society,* it must be taken in this Sense; That if all Religion and Regard, which ought to be had to God's displeasure, were abolished, there would be no Tie left, strong enough to oblige Mankind to a compliance with those Laws and fundamental Constitutions,

Civil Societies were not Instituted for Religions sake.

which are the original Foundation of all Commonwealths; And, that, without the fear of being accountable to God Almighty, no Human Power alone would be prevailing enough to bridle the Enormities of some stubborn and refractory Spirits.

§6. It being therefore beyond question, That Commonwealths were not erected for Religions sake, it is easie to be understood, that the antient Fathers of Families, when they first submitted themselves under a Civil Government, were thereby, not obliged to surrender at the same time, their Religion in the same manner, as they did their Lives and Fortunes to their Sovereigns, for the obtaining the End of Civil Society, which was their common Security. The more, because Religion was not instituted for the obtaining of this mutual Security, and as such, do's not contribute any thing towards the maintaining of Civil Society. Religion arises from a much more noble Spring, than Civil Government; and more strictly obliges Mankind, than any Civil Power; and therefore is unalterable in its Nature. Thus it would be not only useless, but imply a Contradiction; if a Man, who is to become a Subject to a Civil Government, should be obliged to swear Allegiance to his Sovereign, in these following Terms: *J. N. N.* Submit my Will entirely to your Commands; I promise to love, honour, and trust in God, according to your Pleasure; and to put more Confidence in you than in God Almighty; to set aside all your Command, all Love, Respect and Duty, which I owe to God Almighty, and to perform such things as I know to be contrary to him and his Commands. For, here ought to be remembred, what the Apostles said: *We ought to obey God rather than Man.*[17] And, whenever Sovereigns pretend to extend thus far their Authority, they transgress their Bounds; and if they inflict any Punishment on their Subjects, for refusing to be obedient to their Commands, on this Account; such an Act ought to be look'd upon, as illegal, unjust, and tyrannical. God has verified this by extraordinary Miracles: It was an absurd and illegal Proceeding, when *Darius,* overpersuaded by his

Subjects did not submit their Opinions in Matters of Religion, to the Disposal of their Sovereigns.

17. Acts 5:29.

Courtiers, who intended to lay a Trap for *Daniel,* issued out his Proclamation, That *no body, for thirty Days should ask a Petition of any God or Man.*[18] For, what concerns had the King with his Subjects; Prayers (unlawful Prayers, being not accepted of by God Almighty), especially with those made in private? For, if any one should have prayed in publick against the King, it would been a quite different Case; and such a one had deservedly received Punishment, as an Enemy to his Sovereign. Wherefore, *Daniel* did very well, in continuing his daily private Prayers, according to his former Custom; notwithstanding the King's impious and foolish Command; and, was, for this Reason, by an extraordinary Miracle, delivered out of the Lions Den. In the same manner did God preserve *Daniel's* three Companions in the midst of the Flames, because they refused to worship the Golden Image, according to the King's Command:[19] Though, at the same time, it is very probable, that this Image, set up by *Nebuchadnezar,* was not intended to be worshipped as a God; but only as a Sign or Emblem of that Eternal Being, which he would have to be Adored and Worshipped by his Subjects. Certainly, *Jeroboam,* could not be so much besides himself, as to imagine, or to pretend to persuade the Jews, That the Golden Calves, which he had caused to be made,[20] were the same God, by whose Power they were brought out of *Aegypt;* But he set them up as a Token, or Representative, whereby to put them in mind of the Benefits received from God, the great Deliverer of *Israel;* and that they might not want places where to pay their Devotions, and perform their religious Duties. So, that, though he did not fall off from God, but only, for Reasons of State; and because he thought it belonging to his Royal Prerogative, made an Alteration in the outward Form of Worship; Yet was he, with his whole Family, rooted out of *Israel,* and the Jews, for having obeyed and followed their King, in his Idolatry, paid for it with the Loss of the *Holy Land.*[21]

18. Dan. 6:7, 9.
19. Dan. 3:27, 28.
20. 2 Chron. 13:8.
21. Joseph. Arch. 8:3; 2 Kgs. 19:17, 18.

What Power,
according to
the Law of
Nature, be-
longs to
Sovereigns in
Ecclesiastical
Affairs?

§7. Sovereigns are nevertheless, not excluded from having a certain Power and Disposal in Ecclesiastical Affairs, as they are the Supream Heads and Governours of the Commonwealth; and are therefore stil'd, the Publick Fathers, and Fathers of their Native Country. And, as has been said before, as it is one of the Principal parts of Paternal Duty, to implant Piety into their Children; so Sovereigns ought to take care, that Publick Discipline (of which the Reverence due to God Almighty, is one main Point) to be maintained among their Subjects. And, whereas the Fear of God is the Foundation Stone of Probity, and other Moral Vertues; and it being the Interest of Sovereigns, that the same be by all means encouraged in a State; and that Religion is the strongest Knot for the maintaining a true Union betwixt Sovereigns and their Subjects. (God being a God of Truth, who has commanded, that Faith and Compacts should be sacred among Men:) It is therefore a Duty incumbent upon Sovereigns, to take not only effectual Care, that Natural Religion be maintain'd, and cultivated among their Subjects; But they have also a sufficient Authority, to Enact such Laws as may enable them, to keep their Subjects from committing any thing, which tends, either to the total Destruction, or the Subversion, of the Capital Points of Religion: As if, for instance, any one should attempt to deny publickly the Existency of a God, and his Providence, to set up plurality of Gods; to worship fictitious Gods, or Idols in Gods stead, to spread abroad Blasphemies, or to worship the Devil, enter with him into a Compact, and such like Actions. For, if these are kept within the compass of Peoples Thoughts, without breaking out into publick or outward Actions, they are not punishable by the Law, neither can any Humane Power take Cognizance of what is contained only, and hidden in the Heart. And, as to what concerns those Ceremonies which have been annexed to Religious Worship, though it be undeniable, that one of the main Points, towards the maintaining a good Order in the State is, that a due Uniformity, should be observed in the same, Nevertheless, Sovereigns need not be so very anxious on this Account, because these Differences do not Overturn Religion it self; neither do they (as such considered) dispose Subjects to raise Disturbances, and Dissention in the State. Neither can Sovereigns be any great Loosers by the Bargain, if their Subjects differ in some Ceremonies, no more, than if they were divided into several Opinions, concerning some Philosophical Doctrine. But, this is beyond all doubt, that, if under a Religious Pretext, Subjects pretend to raise Factions, which may prove dangerous to the State, or hatch other secret Mischiefs; these are Punishable by the Supream Magistrates, notwithstanding their Religious Pretences; for, as Religion (in its self considered) is not the cause of Vices; so ought it not to serve for a Cloak, wherewith to cover and protect such treacherous Designs. So, the *Roman Senate* did acquit themselves very well in their Station, when they Abolished these Debaucheries, which were crept into the State, with the *Bachanals.*[22] But those Sovereigns, who have transgressed these Bounds, by compelling their Subjects to a Religion of their own Invention, have, without doubt, abused that Power, wherewith they were entrusted. Neither have these Princes acquitted themselves much better in their Station, who have Persecuted their Subjects, for no other Reason, but because they Professed a Religion different from their own, without making a due Enquiry, whether their Doctrine were Erroneous or not. Thus the Proceedings of *Pliny* the Younger, (a Man otherwise of a very good Temper) against the Christians in *Bithynia,* cannot in any wise be justified; For he confesses himself, That he never was present at the Tryals of the Christians; and was therefore ignorant both of their Crime, and consequently, of what Punishment they deserved. For these are his Words: *I only asked some of them several times, whether they were Christians; which they having constantly Professed they were, I ordered them to be carried to the Place of Execution; it being plain to me, That, of what Nature soever their Confession might be, such an inflexible Humour, and obstinate Behaviour, ought not to go unpunished.*[23]

22. The festivals of Bacchus, the wine god. The reputation of these festivals as orgies led in 186 B.C. to a decree by the Roman senate that prohibited the Bacchanalia throughout Italy, except in certain special cases. This is narrated by Titus Livius in his *History of Rome,* book 19, chaps. 8–19. See *Livy,* with an English translation in fourteen volumes, vol. XI, books XXXVIII–XXXIX, translated by Evan T. Sage (London: William Heinemann, 1936), 241–75. [SZu]

23. Pliny (the younger), book X, letter 96. See Pliny, *Letters and Panegyricus in*

Of the
Nature of
revealed
Religion.

§8. But the Condition of Mankind being such, That it was impossible by the sole help of Natural Religion, to attain to that Felicity which was proposed by the great Creator; it had pleased the Great and All-wise God, to reveal unto us Mortals his Will; and to instruct us by what means we may obtain his Favour, and how he expects to be Worshipped by us. It is for this reason, that no body of a right Understanding ought to make the least Scruple, but, that all such Matters as God has revealed to us, in a manner surpassing our Natural Understanding, ought to be reverenced by Mankind, and to be received with a general consent and submission. Among the several Doctrines, thus revealed, the Article of Justification, or the Purging us from Sins through the Merits of our Saviour, was one of the Principal ones. And, I am of Opinion, that these bloody Sacrifices, which from the very Beginning of the World were Instituted by God's Command, were so many Emblems of this our Redemption by the Blood of Christ; for, without this supposition, it would seem scarce Rational, that a living Creature, sensible of Death and Pains, and which cannot be killed without great Torments, should be destroyed for the Honour of its Creator. As if Man should enter into the Work-House of an Artificer, and by destroying his Handy-Work, pretend to do him an extraordinary Honour. This most Antient way of Sacrificing (the chief Badge of True Religion, before it was Corrupted by Ignorance or Superstition) though it was no small addition to Natural Religion; yet did it cause no alteration as to the Exercise of it. For, in the State of Natural Freedom, every one had a right to Sacrifice, though at the same time, every one was not obliged to Sacrifice for himself. For, this Ceremony of Sacrificing being only an Emblem, representing the future Redemption of Mankind, one and the same Sacrifice might answer that End, in respect to all that were present at the time of the Sacrifice. From hence it was become a Custom, that the Heads of each Family used to Sacrifice for the rest; and if more Families were assembled in order to

---

two volumes, vol. II, with an English translation by Betty Radice (London: William Heinemann, 1969), 286–87. [SZu]

Sacrifice, it was to be Administered by him that was chosen by the rest, for that purpose. And it is observable, that the same Person that had the Right of Sacrificing, had also the Power of prescribing time and place for that Sacrifice.[24] Thus when afterwards God had Ordained the Ceremony or Sacrament of Circumcision; *Abraham* did Administer the same in his House, as being the Father of his Family. What we have alledged concerning the Right of Sacrificing, may be proved from thence, that both *Abel* and *Cain,* after they had left their Fathers House, did Sacrifice. And by several Passages in *Genesis,* we are informed, That the Antient Patriarchs (being Fathers of their Families) did erect Altars. So, *Micha* set up a House of Gods at home, during the Anarchy in *Israel,* there being then neither King nor any other Man, that took care of the Publick Worship;[25] thus attributing to himself (though unjustly) the same Right, which the Ancient Fathers of Families had been possess'd of in more Antient Times.

§9. It had pleased God, according to his Wisdom, not to send our Saviour, or the Messias into the World soon after the Creation, at a time when the whole World was not stockt with a sufficient number of Inhabitants; lest his Sufferings might be obliterated by Oblivion, or by a too long Tract of Time, turned into a Fabulous Relation: But he was to appear amongst us, after the whole Earth was filled up every where with Inhabitants, and Mankind was arrived, as it was, to its Age of Perfection. It was also thought convenient, and almost necessary, that the Messias should not appear in this World all upon a sudden, but after his Coming had been long foretold and expected, in order to raise a more ardent desire after him in us Mortals; and that he might find the easier a Reception amongst us, when his Deeds were found so agreeable to what was Prophesied concerning him, so many Ages before. And, that these Predictions or Prophesies might not, through length of time, come to decay, and be buried in Oblivion, God

Amongst the Jews there was a strict Union betwixt the Church and State.

24. Gen. 4:3, 4.
25. Judg. 17:5, 6.

Almighty had in a most peculiar manner, recommended them to the Care and Custody of the Jews, amongst whom, he, as it may be said, kept his Records of Prophesies; it being the most likely, that that same Nation, from whence the Messias was one day to have his Off-spring as Man, upon Earth, would preserve them with their utmost Care, to their great Honour and Advantage. It was questionless in a great measure for this Reason, that God entered with them into so strict a League, Circumcision being made the Badge, whereby to distinguish them from other Nations: And being afterwards become a very numerous People, and freed from the *Aegyptian* Bondage, he himself established at once, both their Civil Government and Religion, (which was not to cease, till the appearing of our Saviour on Earth;) and this in such a manner, that there was always to remain a strict Union betwixt their Religion and State. Therefore the Administration of Religious Worship was committed to one particular Tribe amongst them, unto whom, according to God's special Command, no Lands were allotted, lest they might thereby be inticed to mind Temporal Possessions and Riches, more than God's Service; but were to be maintained out of the Tenths and other Revenues belonging to the Altar in which Sense God is called, *The Portion of the Levites.* There was also a certain place assigned for the Publick Exercise of Divine Worship, with Exclusion of all others; and their whole Religion was thus disposed by God's peculiar Order, that the same could not be put in practice, unless it were in a free Nation, independent from any Foreign Power. This was the true Reason why the Jews, unless they would overturn the Foundation of their Religion, could not be entirely United with any Foreign State. And, as the Jewish Religion and State were of the same Date, their Laws both Ecclesiastical and Civil having been Constituted at the same time, and contained in one Book; so was the Union betwixt their Religion and State, so entire, that the first could not remain standing, after the fall of the last; and therefore the destruction of the Temple, and of the Commonwealth of the Jews, was an infallible Sign of the total abolishment of their Religion. They were called God's People, and the Holy People, because the whole Jewish Nation publickly professed the True Religion.

§10. But, because God himself had Established the Jewish Religion and Ceremonies and fortified them by very severe Laws, no body upon Earth had Power to make the least alteration in them, or to add any thing to, or to diminish from them. The Kings, *Saul* and *Usiah* paid dearly for it, because they attempted to interfere with the Levites in their Office. And those of the Jews that introduced a Foreign Religious Service, are in the Holy Scripture Branded with Infamy. So that their Kings had no further Power in Religious Concerns, than the Supream Inspection, that every one in his Station (not excepting the High Priest himself) did Exercise his Office, according to God's Commands; and that the Ecclesiastical Constitutions were kept inviolable. Neither did the Tribe of *Levi,* or the Priestly Order make up a separate Body independent from the State, but they were actually considered as part of the Nation, and Subjects of their Kings; who, as we read, sometimes Deposed them for several Crimes, and if negligent in their Office, used to give them severe Rebukes. King *David* went further, for he, to maintain a decent Order in the Church, disposed the several Ecclesiastical Functions among the Priests and Levites, and ordered that the Singers and Door-waitors should take their places by Lott, which nevertheless was not done without the Advice of the Chief Men and Elders of the People, and the whole Tribe of *Levi.* In so doing, he did not assume to himself the Power of Disposing or Altering any thing in their Religion, but only over those that were Ordained by God Almighty for that Function, *viz.* to Establish such an Order among them, the better to enable them to Exercise their Function without Confusion.[26] For, when afterwards, instead of the Tabernacle, a Temple was to be Erected, that is to say, when instead of a slight and decayed Building, a most noble and firm Structure was to be built, the same was not undertaken without God's Advice. This Temple being the Principal of all Publick Structures, it was the King's Care to see it Repaired in due time, who also might levy a Tax for that use, and provide for the necessary Expences of the Workmen; it is very remarkable, that we do not read in

Who was the Supream Head of the Jewish Church.

---

26. 4 Chron. 24:3, 4, 5.

the Scriptures, that any of those Kings that introduced Foreign Service among the Jews, did ever attempt to force by Threats, or otherwise, their Subjects to such a Worship, but rather by several Allurements enticed them to follow their Example, and that such as were thus seduced, did, as well as their King, receive Condign Punishment from God, accordingly; And that such among the Jews as abhorred this Idolatry, ought not to be look'd upon as Rebellious Subjects upon that score, but as Persons that did bear this Publick Calamity with Patience. And, as those Kings, that Abolished Idolatry and Foreign Worship amongst the Jews, are highly extolled in the Scriptures, so those Impious Kings, that were the Authors of this Idolatry, were by the high Rank, they bore in the State, exempted from the ordinary Punishment, which according to God's Ordinance, was else to be inflicted upon all others, that should attempt to introduce Idolatry. Lastly, another remarkable Observation may be made as to the Jewish Religion; that, whereas there was so strict an Unity betwixt the State and Religion, that the latter might justly be called the Foundation Stone of the first, and God had expresly enjoyned them an exact observance of it, under forfeiture of the quiet Possession of that Country, where their Commonwealth was Established; the Felicity of the State, depended absolutely from the due observance of that Religion, and the Civil Magistrates were to take cognizance of all such Matters, as might prove either dangerous or destructive to it; as it may plainly appear by the Law of God, prescribed in this behalf, in the Books of *Moses.*

§11. The Christian Religion differs in many points from that of the Jews; not only because it represents our Saviour to us, as he has already appeared upon Earth, and thereby has freed us from these many Ceremonies and Sacrifices, which were so many Emblems of his future coming amongst us; but also, because the Christian Religion is, by God's peculiar Providence, endowed with such Qualifications, that it ought, and may be received by all Nations without Prejudice, and consequently deserves the Name of an Universal Religion; whereas the Divine Worship of the Jews, was so adapted to that State, as scarce to be suitable to any other, being unaccessible to any other Nation but

The Genius of the Christian Religion is quite different from that of the Jews.

their own; the Christian Religion on the other hand, is now-a-days not tyed up to a certain Place or Temple, but every where *Men may pray, lifting up holy hands.*[27] We need not appear before God with sumptuous Sacrifices; but those Sacrifices which are acceptable to God, are to be purchased without Gold or Silver. Neither is the Ministry of the Gospel granted as a peculiar Priviledge to one particular Nation or Family, but the Christians in general are called *Priests before God,*[28] and no body is excluded from that Ministry, provided he be endued with the necessary Qualifications; except that St. *Paul* forbids Women to Teach.[29] Lastly, Each Nation has an equal share in the Christian Religion; neither can any of them claim a peculiar Right or Prerogative before others, every one having equal share in the Merits of Christ. *Here is neither Jew nor Greek; here is neither Bond nor Free, neither Male nor Female; for ye are all one in Christ Jesus.*[30] There is *neither Greek nor Jew, Circumcision, or Uncircumcision, Barbarian, Scythian, Bond nor Free, but Christ is all, and in all.*[31] But because the Christian Religion is not like the Jewish, adapted to one particular State, that had its rise at the same time with this Religion, but was introduced after Civil Societies were erected throughout the World. The main point now in question is, Whether after this Religion has been introduced, it has altered the Nature of Civil Societies, or the Rights of Sovereigns; and whether by its establishment a new sort of Government, separate and independent from the Civil Power, has been introduced? Or, which is the same in effect, Whether the Church is to be considered as a State separate and independent from the Civil Government, which ought to be Governed and Maintained by Human Force and Power? By the Word State, we understand a considerable number of People, who being joyned in one Society, independent from another, are Governed by their own Laws and Governors.

27. 1 Tim. 2:8.
28. Rev. 1:6, 5:10.
29. 1 Tim. 2:12.
30. Gal. 3:28.
31. Coloss. 3:11.

How Moses
behaved him-
self when he
laid the Foun-
dation of the
Jewish Com-
monwealth.

§12. To trace the very Original of this point, the Behaviour of *Moses,* the Founder both of the Jewish Church and State, must be taken into due consideration; and how far different Jesus Christ, the Saviour of Mankind, and Founder of the Christian Church, shewed himself in his Behaviour, from *Moses. Moses* was commanded by God, to deliver the Posterity of the Patriarchs from the *Bondage* of *Aegypt,* and to lead them according to God's Covenant with them, into *Canaan,* the Land of Promise;[32] where he was to Erect a New Commonwealth, and to Establish their Ecclesiastical and Civil Laws at the same time. The better therefore to Establish his Authority not only amongst his Countrymen, (over whom he had no other Lawful Jurisdiction) but also to gain Credit with the *Aegyptians,* that hitherto had kept the others under their jurisdiction; he did, by his Extraordinary and Miraculous Deeds, give them most evident Demonstrations of his Divine Commission, and of a secret Correspondence with God Almighty.[33] These Miracles struck such a Terror into the Aegyptian King, that his Obstinacy was at last overcome; who else, in all likelihood, would not have parted, upon easie terms, with so vast a number of his Subjects; Their number being sufficient to make up a new and strong People: And the Jews moved by his Miracles, and in acknowledgment of the Benefits received from his Hands, and being sensible that *God stood by him in all his Undertakings,* willingly received him for their Prince and General. As long as he lived he exercised this Princely Authority in the highest degree; for, he did Constitute amongst them both their Ecclesiastical and Civil Laws, and Ordained and Established their whole Government. He used to Administer Justice, Inflict Punishments upon those that were found Criminal, he had the Power of Constituting Magistrates and others, that were to aid and assist him in his Office, and those that attempted against his Authority, he made sensible of their Folly, by inflicting most severe Punishments upon them. There was all that time no occasion for the levying of Taxes upon the People, except what was requisite for the Maintenance and Ornament of their Publick

32. Exod. 3:8. [SZu]
33. Exod. 3:11, 20; 4:21; 11:9, 10. [SZu]

Religious Service. He was very watchful for the Preservation of the People, and if they were Attack'd by their Enemies, used to defend them by Force of Arms. Lastly, when he knew that he was shortly to depart this Life, he Constituted his Successor, who was to be their General, and under whose Conduct they were to be put into Possession of the so long desired Land of Promise; from whence it is very evident, that *Moses,* as long as he lived, bore the Office of a Prince, and that he was the Founder of the State or Commonwealth of the Jews.

§13. But if we look upon our Saviour Jesus Christ, he acted in a quite different manner; from whence it was very evident, that his intention was not to Erect a new State here upon Earth. 'Tis true, he gained to himself a great deal of Credit and Authority by his Miracles; but these were no terrifying Miracles, or such as ever proved injurious to any. So, when his Disciples would have persuaded him, to command fire to come down from Heaven, and consume those that refused to receive him, they met with a severe Rebuke.[34] The main Demonstrations he used to give them of his Divinity, always tended to the benefit of others, and the Miracles performed by him, were of such a nature, as must needs attract the love and favour of all Men; and at the same time were apparent and convincing Proofs of his Divinity, not any thing less than a Divine Power being able to cause a new Motion or Alteration in the course of Nature, without Natural means. For *he went about doing good, and healing all that were oppressed of the Devil.*[35] All which had not the least Relation towards the laying of the Foundation of a new State. He had some Disciples, but these were few in number, unarmed, poor, of a mean Profession and Condition, and of so little Authority, that it was impossible for them to make the least pretention of setting up a State of their own, or of raising any Commotions or Disturbances in another State. And when the multitude, in acknowledgment of the benefits received by his Doctrine and Miracles, would at several times have proclaimed him King, he absconded and made his escape. The

What on the other hand our Saviour did, when he established his Church.

34. Luke 9:54, 55.
35. Acts 10:38.

principal Care he took of his Followers, was to instruct them by his Doctrine, from whence they were called Disciples, and they in return, used to give him the Name of Master or Teacher. Neither did he Constitute any new Laws, (at least not any that could be supposed to have any reference towards the Establishment of a new State) but the Antient Law, as far as it was given to Mankind in general, was explained, and the People exhorted to a due observance of it. He did never execute the Office of a Judge,[36] nay he refused to be an Arbitrator, to convince the World that his coming was intended for no such purpose. Lastly, he did himself pay Taxes to others; and, tho' it was in his Power to prevent it, suffered himself to be Judged and Executed. All which is altogether inconsistent with the Nature and Office of a Temporal Sovereign.

Christ did not Constitute a new People.

§14. This will appear more clearly to us, if we duly consider that Christ never acted according to the Rules of those that intend to lay the Foundation of a new State. For, their principal and first care is to Constitute a new People, that is, to bring over to their side such a number of People, as are willing and sufficient to be joyned under one Civil Government. This Multitude of People is either Assembled at once, and drawn out of another Commonwealth, as *Moses* did; or by degrees brought over out of other Commonwealths, as *Romulus* gathered the People of *Rome*. But it is easie to be seen, that our Saviour's Intention was of a quite different Nature. His Disciples were not so many in number, as to have the least resemblance with a Nation or People, neither were they instructed in those matters, which have the least relation to the Establishment of a new Commonwealth. Their dependance from him was not near the same, which Subjects have of their Prince, having never sworn Allegiance to him; but only as Disciples from their Master, being influenced by the Love and Admiration they had both for his Person and Doctrine.[37] Sometimes a great Mul-

36. Luke 12:13, 14; John 8:11.
37. John 6:66, 67, 68.

titude of People would flock about him, but these only came to hear him Preach, and to be Spectators of his Miracles, which being done, they return'd to their respective homes. And Christ never shewed the least inclination to command over, or to withdraw them from the Obedience due to their Sovereigns. Lastly, when the time of his Death approached, his most trusty and particular Friends and Followers absconded, and durst not as much as make any publick appearance. When we therefore speak of Christians, we do not understand a certain Nation or People, subject to any particular Government, but in general, all such, as make profession of a certain Doctrine or Religion.

§15. One of the main points which those that intend to Establish a new Commonwealth ought to take care of, is how to acquire considerable Territories, where their new Subjects may settle themselves and their Fortunes. So, *Moses,* when he saw it not fecible to set up the Jewish Commonwealth within the bounds of *Aegypt,* led them into the Desert, and through such places as were not subject to any particular Government; till such time, that they Conquered the Land of *Canaan,* and rooted out its Antient Inhabitants. Neither were the Jews, before they were put into Possession of this Country, the less free, for they were then a Nation independent from any Foreign Power; and though they sometimes marched upon the Borders of other Princes, nevertheless were they not, during that time, subject to their Jurisdiction; partly, because no body ever laid any particular claim to those Territories, or if some of them did, they marched through them like Soldiers of Fortune, ready to make good their Pretences and Titles to these Lands, by the edge of their Swords. But Christ did say, of himself, *That he was so poor, as he had not where to lay his head.*[38] He was always so far from attempting to acquire any Possessions or Territories, or to encourage his Followers to do it, that he rather chose to live during the whole course of his life in other Territories and under Civil Jurisdiction.

Christ had no Territories belonging to him.

38. Matt. 8:20.

Christ did not exercise the Office of a Prince.

§16. There are a great many other remarkable Circumstances from whence it may plainly be inferred, that Christ never did, nor intended, to appear, as a Prince, here upon Earth. When the Mother of the Sons of *Zebedeus,* begged of our Saviour, that her Sons might be prefer'd to the Chiefest Dignities in the Kingdom of Christ, he rebuked her for her ignorance, and Prophesied to his Followers a very slender share of outward Splendor and temporal Preferments, but abundance of Persecution; nay, he plainly told and enjoyned his Disciples, that they should not strive for Pre-eminency over one another, as Temporal Princes do. *It shall,* says he, *not be so amongst you,* ordering them to live in an equal and Brotherlike degree with one another.[39] And, to remove, by his own Example, all remnants of Pride, he in their presence, did abase himself to that degree of Servitude, as to wash the feet of St. *Peter.*[40] Lastly, it is of great Consequence at the first Establishment of a new Commonwealth, that its Founder be long-lived, that thereby he may be enabled, to lay a more solid Foundation of the new Government. For this reason it was that *David*'s Soldiers would not any longer suffer him to expose his Person in Battel, lest *the light of Israel should be extinguished;*[41] the loss of his own Person being esteemed more than of a great many thousands. But our Saviour did surrender himself voluntarily to death after he had scarce four years appeared in Publick, and that without appointing a Successor, who was to exercise any Power or Authority over those, that followed his Doctrine.

But that of a Doctor or Teacher.

§17. As now Christ, during his abode here upon Earth, did not make the least appearance or outward shew, resembling the greatness of Temporal Princes; and, as out of all his Actions there cannot be gathered the least thing, which may prove his intention to have been to erect a new State or Commonwealth; so it is sufficiently apparent, that, during the whole course of his publick Conversation on Earth, he employed all his Time and Labour in publishing the Word of God. So that in

39. Matt. 20:20ff.
40. John 13:9, 10.
41. 2 Sam. 21:17.

the Quality of a Doctor or Teacher, he appeared to the Eyes of all the World; whereas his Office of being the Saviour of Mankind, was at that time understood, only by such, as were capable of applying the Antient Oracles of the Prophets to his Person.[42] Furthermore, our Saviour to establish and shew his Authority, made use of such Miracles, as might be evident proofs of his Divine Power, partly, because the Antient Ceremonies which were to be abolished, were first ordained by God's special Command; partly, because the principal Heads of his Doctrine were surpassing all Human Understanding. But, as for his way of Teaching, it was plain, and free from Vanity, without all affectation, wherein appeared nothing which justly might cause the least suspicion of fictitious Worship. Notwithstanding his Doctrine appeared thus in her Native and Pure Simplicity, yet, so powerful were its Charm, that all what Human Art, Dexterity, Eloquence has been able to invent of that kind, if compared to the solid Expressions of our Saviour, is only superficial and insipid. Neither do we find, that he made use of any outward means to promote his Doctrine. He did not call to his aid the Power and Authority of Civil Magistates, to force People to receive his Words. The Word was there, *He that can take, let him take it.* And how often do we read that he exclaimed to them, *He that hath Ears to hear, let him hear.*[43] It was not God Almighty's pleasure to pull People head-long into Heaven, or to make use of the new French way of Converting them by Dragoons; But, he has laid open to us the way of our Salvation, in such a manner, as not to have quite debarr'd us from our own choise; so, that if we will be refractory, we may prove the cause of our own Destruction. Neither, did it please Almighty God to inveigle Mankind by the Allurements of Profit and Temporal Pleasures, but rather to foretel those, that should follow his Doctrine, nothing but Adversities, Calamities, Persecutions and all sorts of Afflictions; reserving the chiefest Reward till after this Life, where also such as had neglected his Doctrine, were to receive condign Punishment. This is the most evident Proof that can be given of the

42. John 1:29.
43. Matt. 11:15; 13:9, 43; Luke 8:8; 14:35.

intrinsick Value and extraordinary Worth of the Christian Doctrine; the natural Constitution of Mankind in general, being such as to be chiefly moved with those Objects that are present and affect our Senses; whereas those things that are represented to our Minds at a distance, are but faintly received, and often meet with dubious Interpretations. It is worth our Observation, what Method Christ made use of in his Doctrine, *viz.* That *he taught as one having Authority,* as it is expressed by *Matth. 7:29.* not as the Scribes, that is; he had no recourse to the Authority and Traditions of their Antient *Rabbis,* so as to set up for an Interpreter of their antient Laws, but he spoke Lord-like, and as a Legislator, who had a lawful Authority belonging to himself, to propose his Doctrine. It is my Will and Command, who is it that dare gain-say me? And in this one point only Christ exercised his Regal Power, as well as his Office of Teaching, when he promised great and ample Rewards to all such, as should receive his Doctrine, threatening with Eternal Damnation all those that should refuse to hearken to it. *He that believed not, is condemned already,* are his Words;[44] quite contrary as it is with other speculative Sciences, the Ignorance of which makes no body liable to Punishments. And, in this Sense is to be taken what is related of our Saviour by St. *John;*[45] The reason why the Jews were so bent to the Destruction of Christ, was, because they abominated his Doctrine; nor would they acknowledge him for the same Messias, which was promised so long before. But having at that time no Criminal Jurisdiction belonging to themselves, they were obliged to forge Treason and Rebellion against him, as if his design was to make himself King of the Jews. Jesus therefore being examined by *Pilate* concerning this Accusation, *did not deny it, but witnessed a good Confession,*[46] viz. *That his Kingdom was not of this World,*[47] which is as much as to say; His Kingdom was not like those of Temporal Princes, who exercise Acts of Sovereignty over their Subjects. For, if he had pretended to the

44. John 3:18.
45. John 18:37.
46. 1 Tim. 6:13.
47. John 18:36.

same Prerogatives, he might have commanded his Servants, not his timerous Disciples, but those strong Legions of Angels, who always stand ready to his Command,[48] to protect their Lord from falling into the Hands of *Pilate*. And when *Pilate* replied, *That he then professed himself to be a King,* he answered, That *he was King, but a King of Truth, and that for this cause he came into the World, that he should bear witness unto Truth.*[49] *Pilate,* by what Christ had professed, soon understood that this matter did not fall under his Cognizance, and therefore answered, *What is Truth?* As if he would have said, if nothing else can be objected against you, but that you make profession of Truth, I have no further business with you; for Truth is not subject to any Temporal Jurisdiction. Neither did the Laws of the Roman Empire, wherein so many Nations were comprehended, take any Cognizance at that time, of the various Opinions of their Subjects in matters of Religion, as it plainly appears out of the *Acts,*[50] and out of the Apology of *Athenagoras.*[51] It was for this reason that *Pilate* would have discharged him, if he had not at last thought it more convenient, to appease the rage of the Jews by Sacrificing him, though Innocent, to their Fury. But after Christ had once made this open Confession, he refused to make any further answer to *Pilate,* being sensible that *Pilate* was not desirous to be instructed in this Truth. The Kingdom of Christ therefore, is a Kingdom of Truth, where he, by the force of Truth, brings over our Souls to his Obedience; and this Truth has such powerful Charms, that the Kingdom of Christ needs not to be maintained by the same forcible means and Rules, by which Subjects must be kept in Obedience to the Civil Powers. And for the same reason it is, that there need not be established a particular State, in order to propagate and preserve Truth,

48. Matt. 4:11. [Puf.]
49. John 18:37.
50. Acts 18:14, 15; 26:31. [Puf.]
51. Athenagoras was a Christian apologist from Athens. In c. A.D. 177 he addressed a "message" to the Emperors Marcus Aurelius Antoninus and Lucius Aurelius Commodus in which he defended Christians against charges of atheism, cannibalism, and sexual deviance (*A Plea for the Christians*). See note 187, below. [SZu]

no more, than it is necessary, to set up a separate Commonwealth, where Philosophy and other Sciences are to be taught. For, it is the true Genius of Truth, and such her intrinsick vertue, as to be convincing in it self, provided she be but represented in her genuine Shape; and the fruits, which she produces for the benefit of Mankind, be dexterously proposed to the view of the World. But the divine Truth has, beyond all others, this particular prerogative, that by vertue, and with the assistance of God's Grace our Minds are insensibly drawn into a Belief of those things, that otherwise seem to surpass human Understanding.

The Apostles propagated the Doctrine of Christ.

§18. Christ, after having withdrawn himself from Human Conversation, did Substitute in this Kingdom of Truth his Apostles, but not in the same Rank with himself; not as Kings, but as Ministers and Heralds, to publish his Doctrine. *As my Father, said he, had sent me, even so send I you.*[52] But how had the Father sent him? *viz. To preach the Gospel to the Poor, to heal the broken Hearted, to preach Deliverance to the Captives,* as it is expressed by *Isaiah*[53] and St. *Luke;*[54] So, that the Title of King, of Truth, was a peculiar Title, appertaining to Christ alone. He tells them, *Be you not called Masters, for one is your Master, Christ.*[55] And their Calling was, to Teach all Nations, to observe all things whatsoever Christ had Commanded.[56] St. *Paul* called his Function *a Ministry which he had received of the Lord Jesus, to testifie the Gospel of the Grace of God.*[57] The Apostles had the first Rank among Christ's Followers,[58] but the word Apostle implies as much as a Missionary, or one that is sent by another. So, that they had no other Power or Authority from themselves, to Teach their Doctrine, but to Instruct others in what they had received from Christ. And, when,

52. John 20:21.
53. Isa. 61:1.
54. Luke 4:18.
55. Matt. 23:10.
56. Matt. 28:20.
57. Acts 20:24.
58. Ephes. 4:11.

after the Death of our Saviour, they were quite dejected, and put into a panick Fear, He, by sending the Holy Ghost did so comfort and strengthen them, that they appeared in Publick, and in spite of the *Jews,* and all the Danger that threatned them, preached the Doctrine of the Gospel. But the diversity of Languages being a main obstacle towards the spreading abroad of any Doctrine,[59] the Apostles were by the Holy Ghost upon *Whitsunday,* Endowed with the Gift of speaking various Languages,[60] to enable them, to bring the Nations into one Union of Faith; It being otherwise a Maxim of State received by those that intend to lay the Foundation of a new Commonwealth, to take care, that no more than one Language be used among their Subjects. It is also worth our taking Notice of, that among those Languages which the Apostles spoke,[61] there were Languages of some Nations, that were then Subjects to the *Parthian Empire,* which was at that time in the same degree of Enmity and Hatred with the *Romans,* as may now a days be observed betwixt the *Germans* and *Turks.* Notwithstanding this mortal Hatred betwixt these several Nations, and the difficulties which were to be surmounted in keeping a Correspondence betwixt them, which could not but be a main Obstacle to their being ever united under one Head or Government, the Union of Faith was introduced among them, under the Kingdom of Truth.

§19. The Apostles had nevertheless much more Authority for the exercising of their Functions than others, who profess Human Sciences or Doctrines; For, these cannot pretend to any lawful Authority of Teaching, in publick, unless with Consent, or at least Connivance of the Higher Powers, who may put a stop to them at Pleasure. But the Case is quite different with the Apostles, who having received their Commission of Teaching from Christ, the same cannot be annulled by any Civil Power, so, as to oblige them either to be silent, or to alter their Doctrine, when commanded; neither can they be esteemed dis-

The Apostles had received their Power of teaching from God alone, without any dependance from any Temporal Power.

59. Cor. 14:9, 10.
60. Acts 2:4.
61. Acts 2:9, 10, 11. [Puf.]

obedient or rebellious, if they refuse, in this Point, to follow the Commands of Civil Magistrates. It is very remarkable what Christ spoke to his Apostles by way of Preface, when he was just going to put them into Possession of their Office, These were his Words: *All Power is given unto me in Heaven and in Earth.*[62] And that this Power might not be mistaken for a Temporal Authority, as exercised by Sovereigns over their Subjects, but to be understood of the Power of leading Mankind, and shewing them the true Way to Salvation, plainly appears out of our Saviour's Words, when he speaks thus concerning himself to his heavenly Father: *As thou hast given him power over all Flesh, that he should give eternal Life to as many as thou hast given him. And this is eternal Life, that they might know thee the only true God, and Jesus Christ whom thou hast sent.*[63] And in St. *Luke: He that heared you, heared me, and he that despised you, despised me; and he that despised me, despised him that sent me.*[64] The holy Apostles therefore could not by any Civil Power on Earth be absolved from this Command of Preaching the Doctrine of Christ throughout the World, and Baptizing such as received this Doctrine. They were instructed with the Gift of doing Miracles, as a Proof of their Authority, and Verity of their Doctrine, which being now sufficiently propagated and received by so many, these Miracles are become useless: Like it is the Custom in some Countries, that new Laws are published, under the Sound of Trumpets, which is never repeated after the first Promulgation. They having then received their Authority from Christ, it was a vain Exprobration which was made to St. *Paul* by the *Athenians,* when they said: *What will this Babler say?*[65] Neither could they be justly punished, because they went about to abolish the antiently received Rites and Ceremonies; And when they were commanded to desist from spreading their Doctrine, they might legally refuse to be obedient in this Case; For, *they ought to obey God*

62. Matt. 28:18.
63. John 17:2, 3.
64. Luke 10:16.
65. Acts 17:18.

rather than Men;[66] Nay, they were rather to undergo corporal Punishment, than to renounce the Doctrine of Christ.[67] And those Princes, that violently opposed the Christian Doctrine, are so far from having exercised a legal Civil Authority, that they have rather made themselves guilty of a most enormous Crime against the Divine Majesty, by violating his Legats or Ministers, it being sufficiently known, that publick Ministers, sent by Temporal Princes, are esteemed inviolable.

§20. Besides this Power of Preaching the Gospel, (even in opposition to any Civil Command) there is nothing to be met withal in the whole Apostolical Doctrine, that has the least resemblance of Command or force. 'Tis not to be denied, but that sometimes Teaching cannot so well be performed without something of Force or Command, especially among young People; But this has its off-spring from the Paternal Authority, and is from hence derived unto others. But the Apostles were to Teach whole Nations, such as were independent from others, and past all School Discipline. And what could one single Body, or perhaps two, and that without Weapons, pretend to do by Force against whole Nations and Commonwealths? It was therefore; That the Apostle said: *The Weapons of our Warfare are not carnal, but mighty through God to the pulling down of Strong-holds, casting down Imaginations, and every high thing, that exalted it self against the Knowledge of God; and bringing into captivity every Thought to the obedience of Christ.*[68] And these Weapons are more plainly described in the foregoing 6 *Chap.* to be, *Patience, Tribulations, Necessities, Distresses, Stripes, Imprisonments, Labours, Fastings, Watchings, Pureness, Knowledge, Kindness, the Holy Ghost, unfeigned Love; the Word of Truth, the Power of God, the Armour of Righteousness,* and such like,[69] as may more at large appear out of several places, especially out of the Epistle to the *Ephes.* 6:11, out of

The Apostles never assumed a Power to Command.

66. Acts 4:19, 5:29.
67. Matt. 10:28, 32, 33.
68. 2 Cor. 10:4, 5.
69. 2 Cor. 6:4, 5, 6, 7, 8.

the 2*d*. to the *Corinth*. 8:8, 9:7. to the *Coloss*. 1:23, 25; and out of the
2*d*. to the *Thessal*. 3:12, 14, 15. 'Tis true, in the Parallel of the great
Supper, the Master of the Feast orders his Servants, to go out, and
compel them to come into his House,[70] which is as much to say, as to
oblige them to come in, but not by forcible Means or Threatnings;[71]
or to pull them in by Head and Shoulders, but in such a manner as
was suitable to an invitation to so great a Feast, by Prayers and Ex-
hortations, and making them sensible of the Majesty and Greatness
both of the Master and the Feast. In the same manner as St. *Paul*
expresses it: *We are Ambassadours for Christ, as though God did beseech
you by us; we pray you in Christs stead, be ye reconciled to God.*[72] And,
what can be more evident, than that Ambassadours never pretend to
any Authority over those, unto whom they are sent, but that their
Negotiations ought to be accomplished by force of Reason and Per-
swasions. The word also of *feeding*, which is used by St. *John* implies
nothing of Command, but only the due Administration of Food; especially, since our Saviour told expresly to *Peter, Feed my sheep*, not
thine;[73] lest he should be apt to imagine by the said words, he had
liberty given him to use his Flock according to his own Discretion;
But, to make him sensible, he was bound up to the same Rules, which
the Patriarch *Jacob* had formerly prescribed to himself.[74] Lastly, our
Saviour is very plain in this Point, when he says: And *whosoever shall
not receive you, nor hear your Words, when you depart out of that House
or City, shake off the Dust of your Feet, leaving them to receive condign
Punishment for this Contempt of the Gospel, at the Day of Judgment.*[75]

70. Luke 14:3.

71. The Huguenot Pierre Bayle took these words of Jesus as a starting point to
demonstrate that there is nothing more abject than making people convert by force.
See his *Commentaire philosophique sur les paroles de Jésus Christ "Contrains-les
d'entrer,"* translated as *A Philosophical Commentary on the Words of the Gospel, Luke
XIV: 23, "Compel them to come in, that my House may be full"* (1708), reedited by J.
Kilcullen and C. Kukathas (Indianapolis, Ind.: Liberty Fund, forthcoming). [SZu]

72. 2 Cor. 5:20.

73. John 21:17.

74. Gen. 31:38, 39, 40.

75. Matt. 10:14, 23.

This was actually performed by St. *Paul* at *Antiocha,* and *Corinth.*[76] But those Rules which are prescribed in the 1 Epistle to the *Corinthians,* Chap. 11, from *v.* 2, to 22, 23, 24; and 1 *Corinth.* Chap. 14; as also in *Tim.* 2:8 *Ver. Chap.* 5:9 *Ver.* and some other passages of the same nature, do not imply any Command or Legislative Power, but are only Moral Precepts, and Points of Doctrine.

§21. But it may perhaps be objected, That the Apostles and their Successors, might at least by indirect ways and means, exercise an Authority over Christians, *viz.* by denying them the Doctrine of the Gospel, which shews Men the way to Salvation, unless they would in other Matters also submit themselves to their Authority. For, who would not rather submit to any thing than to be deprived of that Doctrine, which leads us to Heaven, and frees us from eternal Punishment? But it cannot in the least be supposed, that such Extortions could ever enter into the Apostles Thoughts, who joyfully gave for nothing, what they had received for nothing, and judged it a heinous Offence in *Simon,* who pretended to make a Trade of the Gospel. St. *Paul* says: *Though I preach the Gospel, I have nothing to glory of, for Necessity is laid upon me; yea, wo is unto me, if I preach not the Gospel.*[77] Neither do I see, which way they could have made their market by the Gospel. For, what is not understood, is not valued; if therefore they would raise in the People a desire to the Gospel, it must of necessity be first taught them. Neither is there any Reason to suppose, that the same Men, who rather would loose their Lives than neglect their Divine Commission, should be guilty of so hainous a Crime. And the Doctrine of the Gospel, being now a-days sufficiently spread abroad, it would be in vain for the Clergy of one Province or Commonwealth, to deny the Doctrine of the Gospel to its Inhabitants, in case they would not comply with their Demands; since, if they should persist in their Folly, there would not be wanting such as would supply their Places without reluctancy. Neither did Christ absolutely commit his Doctrine to the sole Management of the

Whether the power of Teaching does indirectly imply any Command.

76. Acts 13:51, 18:6.
77. 1 Cor. 9:16.

Priests, in such a manner, as by Tradition to be transplanted from one to another; but, he ordered it to be put in Writing, not to be kept close up by any one certain Colledge or Society, who were invested with a particular Prerogative to look into it, like it was at *Rome,* with the *Sybilline* Oracles;[78] and granted a general Priviledge for every Body to peruse it, and to instruct themselves in the Christian Doctrine, and in such other Points as belonged to the Ministry of the Gospel. But if a foreign Priest should attempt to forbid the exercise of Religious Worship in another Commonwealth, scarce any body, unless quite prepossessed with Superstition, would make the least account of it. The *Venetian* Commonwealth has given us a notable instance of this Nature in our Age; For, tho' the *Venetians* are *Roman Catholicks,* nevertheless did they oblige their Priests to exercise the Ministerial Function, in spite of the Pope's Commands to the contrary.

Whether the power of Absolution imply's any right to a Sovereignty?
§22. It seems to be a Matter of the greatest Consequence, and therefore the more to be taken notice of, when it is said: That our Saviour *did give the Keys of the Kingdom of Heaven to St. Peter,* and the rest of his Apostles; so, that, *whatsoever they should bind on Earth, shall be bound in Heaven; and whatsoever they should loosen on Earth, shall be loosened in Heaven.*[79] The whole Matter, duely examined, appears to be of the highest moment, *viz.* to have the Power of excluding Sinners from the Kingdom of Heaven, and of admiting such as are freed by their Ab-

78. Pufendorf speaks of the "Sibylline Books" (libri Sibyllini). This collection of sibylline prophecies was offered for sale to Tarquinius Superbus, the last of the seven kings of Rome, by the Cumaean sibyl, a legendary prophetess. He refused to pay her price, so the sibyl burned six of the books before finally selling him the remaining ones. The books were kept in the temple of Jupiter on the Capitoline Hill, to be consulted by a committee first of two, later of ten, and eventually of fifteen priests on official request by the Senate. The translator obviously confused the Sibylline Books with the Sibylline Oracles. The latter consist of a collection of oracular prophecies in which Jewish or Christian doctrines were allegedly confirmed by a sibyl, that is, a legendary Greek prophetess. The prophecies were actually the work of certain Jewish and Christian writers from about 150 B.C. to about A.D. 180. [SZu]

79. Matt. 16:19; John 20:13.

solution; for what is it, that may not be obtained from a Sinner in this case, especially if the Priest refuse him Absolution, unless he promises a blind Obedience to his Demands? It ought therefore to be taken into serious consideration, what is the true meaning of this Metaphorical Locution, *viz.* The Keys of the Kingdom of Heaven; since the same admits of divers Explications in the holy Scripture. In the *Rev.* 1:18. the Son of God says of himself, That *he has the Keys of Hell and of Death,* which is explained by some, that he has the Power of inflicting Punishment, as if he would say: *I have power to destroy both Soul and Body in Hell,* as it is expressed in St. *Matthew* 10:28. Tho' by this also might be understood, the power of delivering from Death and Hell, and to destroy the force of Death and Hell. It is also spoke of the *Scribes,* That *they have the Key of Knowledge,*[80] which is by some applied to their Function of Teaching Wisdom to others. Tho' this may also be understood from the holy Scripture it self, the true Spring of Knowledge and Wisdom, the Interpretation of which did in a most peculiar manner belong to their Function. In the Book of *Revelation,* the Son of God is said *to have the Key of David, that he opened, and no Man shutteth, and shutted, and no man opened.*[81] And in the 22th *Chapter* of *Isaiah,* it is said of *Eliakim,* the Son of *Hilkiah; That the Key of the House of David shall be laid upon his Shoulder; so, that he shall open, and none shall shut; and he shall shut, and none shall open.*[82] Where the word, *Key,* cannot be taken for an absolute or despotick Power, but for a Ministerial Function; like to that of a Steward, such a one as St. *Paul* had professed himself, and his Fellow Apostles.[83] Out of these several places, if duely compared, this general Assertion may be made, that, to have the Keys of a certain thing, is as much as to say, to have the means to attain, or to come to it. But how far these Means are at our disposal, and what use ought to be made of them, must be gathered out of other Circumstances.

What is to be understood by the Keys of the Kingdom of Heaven.

80. Luke 11:52.
81. Rev. 3:7, 9:1.
82. Isa. 22:22.
83. 1 Cor. 4:1.

What is to
be understood
by absolving
from Sins.
§23. Furthermore, it is to be considered, That the use of these Keys is appropriated to the binding and forgiving of Sins: For as soon as our Sins are taken away, (or which is the same in effect) if our Sins are forgiven, (other Means of Salvation being not neglected) the Kingdom of Heaven is open to us. But as long as the Sins remain upon us, and produce their pernicious Effects, the Kingdom of Heaven is shut up against us, nothing of unclean being to enter there. If therefore a true Judgment is to be given, of what share of Power the Apostles had in forgiving, and retaining of Sins, a due enquiry must be made, of what is to be understood, by forgiving and retaining of Sins? He, that does an unjust Act, commits an Offence both against the Legislator, whose Authority is thereby violated, and against him, who is damnified by it. Besides this, there are some Offences of such a Nature, as to touch whole Societies, as far as their Reputation is thereby impair'd, the Crime committed by one of their Members, being oftentimes attributed to the whole Body. It is therefore from the Damage, which the Legislator, a single Person, or whole Society, receive by such an Offence, that an Action lies, against the Offender; In the same manner as a Creditor has a right to sue his Debtor for a Debt, contracted with him. In which respect it is, that Sins are often called Debts in the holy Scripture. But, in this double, or sometimes, threefold Action, which arises from one Offence committed against several Persons, each is to be considered as separate from the other; so, that, tho' one Action be taken off, the other remains notwithstanding this, in full force: For, as God does not remit Sins, without Satisfaction given from the Offender, to the offended Person;[84] So, tho' the Offender be reconciled to the offended, nevertheless is he obliged to seek for Remission of his Sin by God; And, if the Offence be hainous, and of such a Nature, as to be scandalous to a whole Society, he ought there, also to endeavour his Reconciliation, by begging forgiveness of them. Therefore, to remit a Sin, is the same Thing, as to remit an Action, or to release one from

84. Matt. 5:23, 24.

an Action, which the offended Party had against the Offender. And
he, that has an Action against another, by reason of some Offence
committed against him, may properly be said, to have Power to remit
that Offence or Sin, as far as his Action reaches. For, God himself does
not make use of his uncontrouled Power of remitting of Sins; so, as
without any further Respect, and by his mere Pleasure to remit their
Sins to some, and to punish others. For, to pardon Offences promis-
cuously, without any further regard but bare Pleasure, is in effect to
render Laws ineffectual; and Laws are made to no purpose by him,
who at the same time grants a License of Trespassing against them.[85]
And, because it was beyond all Human Power to give Satisfaction to
God Almighty for our Offences, our Saviour Jesus Christ has made
use of a most wonderful Moderation betwixt Justice and Mercy, in
giving due Satisfaction in his own Person; So, that, whoever by the
Faith appropriates the same to himself, thereby obtains Remission of
his Sins from God. And, as to that part, which belongs to Men to
forgive, God has commanded them not to be rigorous, if the Offender
beg forgiveness, because every one of us must every day expect Forgiveness of his Sins from God Almighty; and we all commit sometimes
Offences against our Neighbours, who, if they would all act rigorously
with us, our Condition would be most deplorable. Wherefore we ought
to forgive our Debts; as we would have others forgive us their Debts.[86]
Neither are we to be too rigorous against such Sinners, as have by their
Offences proved scandalous to a whole Society, but if they seriously
repent, we ought not to deny them our Pardon.[87] It is also worth our
further Observation, That the following Words; *Verily I say unto you,*
whatsoever you shall bind on Earth, shall be bound in Heaven, and what-
soever you shall loosen on Earth, shall be loosened in Heaven, are spoken
by Christ also of the Remission of an Offence by the Party offended;[88]

85. Hebr. 9:22; Matt. 5:18. [Puf.]
86. Matt. 6:12, 14, 15; 5:25; 18:21ff.
87. 2 Cor. 2:6, 7, 8.
88. Matt. 18:18.

Neither does the Sense of the preceding Words allow to apply them only to his Disciples, they being spoken not only to the Apostles, but to the Believers in general.

Under whose name and authority the Apostles did exercise this power of Absolution.

§24. Supposing then that the Apostles were to remit such Sins as were not committed against them, it must necessarily follow, That they, when they remitted Sins, did it either in the name of such particular Persons, against whom the said Sins were committed, or in the name of a whole Society, or else in the name of some (Human or Divine) Legislator. Now it is certain, that no body can remit another Man's lawful Action, without his order or consent, no more than you can lawfully take away another's Right or Property; and therefore it is absolutely necessary, first, to make our peace with the Person offended; without which, we ought not to seek for Pardon from God Almighty; at least, he, that has offended ought to take first, a firm Resolution, to give Satisfaction, as far as is in his Power. Christ says; *First, be reconciled to thy Brother, and then come and offer thy Gift.*[89] And St. *Paul* offered to make Satisfaction to *Philemon,* for what Damage he had received from *Onesimus.*[90] From hence arises that general and common Rule: That *if Restitution be not made, there can be no Remission of the Sin.* For, it is ridiculous, and a contradiction in it self, to profess to God Almighty a true Repentance for an unjust Act, and at the same time enjoy the benefit of it. But, as for the Remission of such enormous Crimes as were committed against a whole Society, the Apostles had their share in it, as is evident out of the 1 Epistle to the *Corinth. c.* 5:4, 5. and 2 *Corinth. c.* 2:10. *c.* 11:29. and will be more treated of hereafter. It will be sufficient in this place to take notice, that what Authority was exercised by them in this kind, was much inferior to that power which they had received of Retaining and Forgiving of Sins. But to remit Sins in the name of those that had the Sovereign and Legislative Power in the State, did not belong to the Apostles, their Commission and Power being not to interfer with the Civil Jurisdic-

89. Matt. 5:24. See also Luke 19:8.
90. Philem. 1:19. [Puf.]

tion, or to diminish its Prerogatives; Wherefore Civil Magistrates justly may, and do punish, Offenders according to the Laws of the Realm, notwithstanding they have made their peace with God. The only way then for the Apostles was, to forgive Sins in the Name of God, by whose Authority they had received their Commission, as is evident out of these Words: *Whatsoever you shall bind on Earth, shall be bound in Heaven, and whatsoever you shall loosen on Earth, shall be loosened in Heaven.*[91]

§25. But, if we propose to form to our selves a true Idea of the Power granted to the Apostles, when the Keys of the Kingdom of Heaven were given unto them, and how far it extends it self, we must take into serious Consideration, in what manner Christ himself did remit Sins, whilst he lived among us upon Earth. This is sufficiently manifest out of several Passages in St. *Matthew,* 9:2. *Mark,* 2:3. *Luke,* 5:20. *c.* 7:47, 48, 49, 50. where our Saviour verifies his Power of forgiving of Sins, by a Miracle, which could not but be the effect of a Divine Power. Besides this, there was no Plaintiff or Defendant, there was no open or express Confession of Sin; but as soon as Christ saw their Faith, he pronounced Remission of Sin. And, if we peruse the whole New Testament, it will most evidently appear, that neither Christ nor his Apostles did forgive Sins in a judicial way, where Crimes are first examined; but where the Faith was, the forgiveness of Sins was the immediate consequence of it. *He that believed in him,* says St. *John, is not condemned, but he that believed not, is condemned already.*[92] Neither is that Confession (whether tacit or express) which ought to precede the Remission of Sins, like to those Confessions, which in Judicial Courts are required to be made by Offenders, and are sure to meet with deserved Punishment; But it has a resemblance to those Confessions, that are made to Physicians, by such of their Patients as labour under a secret Distemper, hoping thereby for Relief in their Diseases. As it is expressed in the 32 *Psalm, v.* 3, 4, 5. of *David;* Neither can true Repentance be

Of what nature this Power was.

91. Matt. 16:19, 18:18. [SZu]
92. John 3:18.

supposed without such a Confession; for, how can we ask forgiveness either of God, or our Neighbour, whom we have offended, unless we confess and acknowledge our Error.[93] Lastly, it is to be observed, That Christ and his Apostles, during the time of Grace, here upon Earth, did not intend to set up a judicial Court, but to preach, and to announce repentance and forgiveness of Sins. But of the great Day of judgment, it is said, That God will proceed to Judgment in a solemn manner, there, *the Supream Judge will sit upon the Throne of Judgment; there Seats are to be prepared for the Assessours, the Books are to be opened, and every one is to be judged according to his Works;*[94] and that without Appeal: It ought also to be taken notice of, That, tho' we have obtained pardon for an Offence from our Neighbour, this does not always and necessarily imply a Pardon from God Almighty; for it is possible, that, notwithstanding a Pardon obtained from Men, God has not absolved us from that Offence; as for instance, if the Offender be without true Faith, or an Hypocrite: And, on the other hand, it is possible that our Offences are forgiven by God, when forgiveness has been denied us by Men; as in case, our Neighbour refuses to pardon an Offence, tho' we beg Forgiveness, and profer Satisfaction to be made; or, a Priest, being overcome by private Passion, should deny us Absolution; When therefore the Priest says; *Thy Sins are forgiven unto thee,* it is not always to be taken for granted, that Christ does then make use of the same Words; For, God alone is the Judge of our Faith, and even our Thoughts; But Men can only give their Judgment according to such Circumstances, or outward Signs, as effect our Senses, which often prove deceitful, and far different from what we keep concealed within us. And, tho' in Civil Courts of Judicature it is sufficient, if Judgment be given in a Case, according to what is proved by Evidence, notwithstanding the same may be contrary to Truth; it is quite otherwise with God Almighty, who, searching into the very bottom of our Hearts, cannot be deceived by Hypocrisie. And, tho' the Priest should tell thee a hundred times over and over, thy Sins are forgiven unto thee, and

93. Prov. 28:13. (1 John 1:9; Jam. 5:16. [Puf.])
94. Rev. 20:12.

thou art destitute of Faith, it can avail thee nothing. Lastly, it ought not to be forgotten, that, when God did give unto the Apostles the Keys of the Kingdom of Heaven, he did not thereby surrender all his Power of forgiving Sins, or of receiving penitent Sinners into his Favour; or did debar himself from making use of this Power, unless by the means of Priests, so as to reserve only to himself the Supream Prerogative of remitting of Sins, in case of an unjust refusal of the Priest; No, by no means; for if this were granted, it would be in vain for us to pray every day; *Forgive us our Sins.* All these things duely considered, are evident Proofs, that, when it is said, that the Keys of the Kingdom of Heaven were given unto the Apostles, it is to be understood from the Doctrine of the Gospel, which treats of the remission of Sins through our Faith in Christ; when the Apostles taught this Doctrine to the Believers, it was said of them, that they forgave Sins, in the same sense as they are said to save others by Preaching the Gospel to the Believers.[95] And on the contrary, when they preach the Gospel to the Unbelieving, they are said to have bound them, so, as that they shall be bound in Heaven.[96] The Apostles therefore, when they announced to the Believing the Grace of God and Forgiveness of Sins through Christ, did open the Gates of Heaven; and they shut them against such, as, being unbelieving, refused to accept this Doctrine. So, that, when a Minister of the Church applies this Doctrine of the Gospel to one particular Person, he says thus much to him: *If thou believest according to thy Confession, I announce and confirm unto thee Remission of thy Sins, through the Merits of Christ; so, that thou mayest be now assured, that the same are forgiven by Christ in Heaven: But if thou not believest, thy Sins are not forgiven.* For, remission of Sins is the necessary consequence of Faith, even before the Absolution is pronounced by the Priest; it being not left to the arbitrary Pleasure of Men, whether to apply the gracious Doctrine of Remission of Sins to a believing Person, or not; But, he that believes, is thereby justified before God, notwithstanding he be prevented from receiving Absolution from the

95. 1 Tim. 4:16.
96. John 3:18.

Priest. Out of what has been said, it is evident, that, according to the Intention of our Saviour, these Keys of the Kingdom of Heaven were not to be made use of for the Establishment of a Temporal State, or to gain other Temporal Advantages. For, Christ ordered the Apostles to preach Remission of Sins, and give for nothing, what they had received for nothing; but not to traffick with the Word of God. Neither did they, by preaching the Gospel, make Men subject to themselves, but to Christ; Nay, St. *Paul,* could not understand without Indignation, that some among the *Corinthians* would be called from him, some from *Apollo,* &c.[97]

Whether St. Peter had any Prerogative granted him before the rest of the Apostles?

§26. But of what nature soever their Power or Function might be, the same was granted in an equal degree to all the Apostles, so, that none of them could claim a particular Prerogative, or, at least not any right of Commanding the rest. For, if we peruse those several Passages in the holy Scripture, where the Apostolical Function was established, and conferred upon them, there are not the least footsteps of Inequality to be found among them. And that Passage *St. Luke* 22:26, 27. Epistle to the *Galat.* 2:9, 14. By *St. Matth.* 16:18. which the *Romanists*[98] make such a stir about,[99] contains nothing, that can give any legal Pretence of Superiority to St. *Peter,* and much less to the *Roman* Bishops over all the Christian Churches. St. *Peter* had in the abovementioned place made his Confession, That *Jesus was the Son of the living God.*[100] This excellent Confession did deserve a suitable answer from Christ, who said, thou art *Peter,* as if he would say, persist in this thy Confession *Peter;* which does in no wise imply, that *Peter* should thereby have deserved those Prerogatives over the other Apostles, as the *Romanists* do pretend to. For, St. *Peter* did not make this Confession for himself only, but in the Name of all those, unto whom Christ spoke at that time. In the same manner as he spoke in the Name of the rest of the

---

97. 1 Cor. 1:12, 13.
98. The Roman Catholics. [SZu]
99. Matt. 28:18, 19, 20; John 20:21, 22, 23; Matt. 23:8ff.; John 13:14.
100. Matt. 16:16. [SZu]

Disciples by St. *John* 6:69. *We believe, and are sure, that thou art Christ the Son of the living God.* Neither was *Peter* the first, that made this Confession; For, before him the same had been made by *John* the Baptist,[101] by St. *Andrew,*[102] *Philip*[103] and *Nathaniel.*[104] And it is no difficult Task to prove out of several passages of the holy Scripture, that none could be taken for a true Disciple of Christ, unless he had made this Confession;[105] And our Saviour, to shew, of what consequence this Confession was, added these Words: *Upon this Rock I will build my Church.*[106] Which is as much as to say, this Doctrine, that Jesus is the Son of God, is the main Foundation Stone, whereupon is to be built the mystical Edifice of the Christian Church. So, that no further inference can be made from these Words, than what is expressed to the same purpose by St. *John,* 20:31, and in the 1 Epist. of *John,* 2:22. *c.* 3:20. *c.* 4:2. *viz.* That the fundamental Article of the Christian Religion is: *That Jesus of Nazareth is the true Messias, and the Son of the living God.*

§27. It also is worth our Consideration, whether the Power of Excommunication, which was used by the Apostles, and in the Primitive Church, implies any Sovereign Authority, such as ought to be exercised in a State? Unto this we answer in the Negative; provided the same be taken according to the proper Use and End of its genuine and primitive Institution. For, that this Power may with conveniency enough, be made use of, (if misapplied) to serve an ambitious Design, and to keep the poor People in awe, is sufficiently proved by Experience. It seems to me, that there was a remarkable Difference betwixt the Excommunication of the Jews, by virtue of which they were excluded from their Synagogues, and the Excommunication used among the Primitive Christians. For, among the Jews, where the Sovereigns and the People

Whether the Power of Excommunication implies any Sovereign Right or Jurisdiction.

101. John 1:34, 36.
102. John 1:42.
103. John 1:45.
104. John 1:49.
105. Matt. 10:32, 33; John 11:27; Acts 4:12; 8:37; 9:20, 22.
106. Matt. 16:18. [SZu]

professed one and the same Religion (which also was entirely united with the State) it might easily happen, that the Exclusion from the Synagogue, did carry along with it several Inconveniencies in Civil Affairs, and might therefore not unjustly be considered at the same time, as a Civil Punishment; which, rendered the Offenders infamous in the Commonwealth; Especially, since, according to the Fundamental Constitution of that Government, there were several things belonging to Religion punishable by their civil Constitutions. But, it being already put beyond Question, that neither our Saviour, nor his Apostles, did ever pretend to any Civil Power; and that besides this, the Primitive Christians lived under the Jurisdiction of other Princes, how could their Excommunication, Ban, or what other sort of Ecclesiastical Censure was used among them, be supposed to have any influence upon the Civil State and Condition of the Christians; or to have been of the same nature and force (properly speaking) as Civil Punishments are? This will more plainly appear, if we examine those Passages, where this Matter is compleatly treated of in the New Testament: It is said in *Matthew* 18:15, 16, 17. *If thy Brother shall trespass against thee, go, and tell him his Fault, between thee and him alone; If he shall hear thee, thou hast gained thy Brother. But, if he will not hear thee, then take with thee One or Two more, that in the mouth of two or three Witnesses every Word may be established. And if he shall neglect to hear them, tell it unto the Church, but if he neglect to hear the Church, let him be unto thee as a Heathen Man and a Publican.* Certainly out of this passage, nothing can be inferr'd that has any relation to a Temporal Jurisdiction or Sovereignty; but barely shews us, how differences ought to be composed among Christians. So St. *Paul* ordains, that we shall rather leave Differences to the Arbitration of a Brother, or rather take wrong, than to go to Law with a Brother before the Unbelievers, to the great shame of the Christian Name.[107] So, that, tho' it is else required from the Offender to beg the Pardon of, and offer Satisfaction to the Person offended; nevertheless, if he neglect his Duty in this Point, Christ commanded, that the offended Party shall first offer a Reconciliation,[108]

107. 1 Cor. 6:1, 2. See also Matt. 5:40.
108. Mark 11:25; Luke 6:27; Acts 7:60. [Puf.]

and try before he brings his Action against the Offender, whether Satisfaction for the Injury received, and a Reconciliation may not be obtained by a private Arbitration. If this prove fruitless, he says, he ought to take along with him two or three Witnesses, to try whether they can prevail with his Adversary to bring him to a more pliable Temper; and at the same time, may testifie, That the offended Party, did offer every thing which might tend towards a Reconciliation betwixt them; But, if after all this, he remain obstinate, the Difference ought to be referr'd to the whole Congregation of the Believers, residing in that Place; (for I see no reason why by the word *Ecclesia* or Church, the *Presbyters* only should be understood.) But, if they also cannot prevail with their Authority over his Stubborness, let him then be unto thee like a Heathen man and Publican, unto whom his Trespasses will not be remitted, because he refuses to acknowledge his Offence, or to give Satisfaction for it; which is as much as to say, fly his Conversation, like that of a vile Person; which every one may freely do, without being thereunto compelled by any Superior Power. For, that the Jews did not converse with the Heathens and Publicans, except in Civil Affairs, is of no great force against us, it being certain, that the Heathens and Publicans were not so infamous in themselves by any Civil Constitution, the Jews being at that time subject to the Heathens, who matter'd not their Conversation. Besides this, it is left to every ones free Choice, whom he will admit into his familiar Conversation; and always was a certain Rule among the wiser Sort, not to be familiar with People of a perversed Humour, and an ill Life, whose Conversation every body may avoid, as he finds it most convenient. So, the Apostle bids us, to reject a Man that is a Heretick, after the first and second Admonition,[109] lest we should be infected with his false Doctrine, for which he is to expect due Punishment from God Almighty.[110] Neither does that passage, in the 1 Epistle to the *Corinthians,* 5:1. and following Verses, and in the 2 Epistle to the *Corinthians,* 13:2, 10. where St. *Paul* declares, that according to the Power given him, he intends to deliver the incestuous Person to Satan, (take it in what sense you please) involve any Civil

109. Tit. 3:10; 2 Thess. 2:14.
110. 2 Pet. 2:1, 2; Gal. 1:8, 9.

Jurisdiction or Command; no more, than those in the 1 Epistle to the *Corinthians*, 6:9. *seq.* in the 1 *Timothy*, 1:20. in the 2 Epist. of *John*, 5:10. All which passages signifie no more, than that every body may freely decline the Conversation of such People, as he thinks may be reproach, or hurtful to him, without implying a prejudice to their Reputation in Civil Affairs. So, that, by avoiding the Conversation of ill Livers, we are not obliged to retire from the World; that is, we need not be so scrupulous in avoiding such Conversation, as to neglect our Duty, or other necessary Business appertaining to Civil Society. And in this sense it is appliable as well to Christians, as to Pagans, of an ill Conversation.

§28. Lastly, if we cast our eyes upon those Instructions, which Christ gave to his Apostles and Disciples, it will evidently appear, that their Commission had not the least relation to the Establishment of a Sovereign State. A State cannot be without a Supream Head, who having Power to bestow Honours and Dignities, this generally proves the occasion of ambitious Designs. A State cannot be maintained without considerable Revenues, which entices Men to Avarice. But, if we look upon our Saviour, we shall find that his main Endeavour is to keep his Disciples from ambitious Designs and Covetousness.[111] The Instruction given by Christ to his Disciples in S. *Matthew* 10. when, after having endowed them with the Gift of Miracles, he sent them, as it was, to make their first Tryal, among the Jews, deserves particularly here to be taken notice of; tho' it is not to be questioned, but that the same Instruction remained in force for the most part, after they were sent among the Gentiles. The first Precept in this Instruction is, That they shall take heed not to abuse the Christian Doctrine, and the Gift of Miracles for the heaping up of Gold and Silver, which are otherwise accounted the Sinews of a State. As you have received it for nothing, so you shall give it for nothing, is the Command, which was very well observed by *St. Peter*, when he said, *Silver and Gold have I none.*[112]

The Commission of the Apostles contains nothing resembling any Sovereign Power.

---

111. Matt. 18:1, 2, 3, 4; Mark 9:33ff.; Luke 9:46; John 13:13, 14.
112. Acts 3:6.

And, lest they should, under pretence of Subsistance and acquiring Necessaries, be enticed to Avarice, Christ forbid them, even to provide two Coats, Shoes, Staves, or a Purse; but that they should be contented with what they received from their Auditors. It is not to be denied, but that this Command may chiefly be applied to such Journeys, as were not to be too long, or in far distant Countries; But on the other hand it ought to be taken into consideration, that the Allowances, to be given to those that preached the Gospel, are compared to the Wages of Workmen, which seldom amount to any more, than is necessary for Subsistance; or, at the most, cannot exceed a private Fortune, having not the least comparison with those vast Revenues, which are required to maintain a State. As may be seen in *Mat.* 10:10. *Luk.* 10:7. 1 *Cor.* 9:11. And the passage in the 1 Epist. to *Timothy* 5:18. chiefly relates to the Priesthood, where it is expressly forbidden not to make a Trade of their Office, and to fly Avarice, as the root of all Evil; and consequently of all those Abuses and Superstitions, which have overwhelmed the Church of *Rome,* And, that by their Number they might not appear terrible, Christ only sends them two and two,[113] with this express Command, not to force their Doctrine upon any Body, but to seek for reception by a kind Salute, and, if they find them inclined to receive their Doctrine, to abide there, but to leave those, whom they found unworthy, and not ready to hear their Words, and even to shake off the Dust of their Feet: After these instructions are given, Christ foretels them what Persecutions and Dangers they must undergo, all which, he will have them to overcome, not by Force, but by Patience, by shewing their Innocence, or flying to another Place.[114] The quite contrary is practiced in Temporal Governments, whose Founders lay this down for a sure Maxim of State, *Tu contra audentior ito, Never shrink before your Enemy.* After the Ascension of our Saviour, they dispersed into all Parts of the World according as they were inspired, without having appointed any certain place of Residence for their Government, from whence they might receive their Instructions or Commissions,

113. Mark 6:7.
114. Matt. 5:10, 11.

and where they were to be accountable concerning their Negotiation, or where to fix the Center of their Correspondency; at least, thus much is certain, that nothing like it is recorded in the holy Scripture. Neither was it in their Power to have acquired any great Territories, it being obvious, that they lived always under another Jurisdiction, and in such Places, where the Government was already Established. Nor had they any Authority to exact upon their Auditors, except what they were pleased to allot them by voluntary Contribution; For, if they should have attempted any thing beyond it, no doubt but those Magistrates, under whose Jurisdiction they lived, might legally have stopt their Proceedings, as done in prejudice of their Authority. For, in case the generality, or the greatest part of the Christians should have attempted to follow the Example of some of their Brethren at *Jerusalem,* who were for having all things in Common,[115] it had been lawful for their Sovereigns to put a stop to their inconsiderate Design, which needs must have tended to the great detriment of the Commonwealth. Lastly, the Apostles did not oblige their Auditors to leave their antient Habitations, like *Moses* led the *Israelites* out of *Aegypt,* but left them in quiet Possession of their former Station and honest Functions, not pretending to any Innovation, but that they should receive the Christian Religion.

The Kingdom of Christ implies no Temporal Sovereignty. §29. It is furthermore to be considered, whether the Doctrine of Christ, which unites our Hearts under the Obedience of Christ by the Faith, does not, by vertue of this Union, constitute a certain Sovereignty resembling the Sovereign Power of our Civil Governments? To this we answer in the Negative; as it may plainly appear, to those, that will duely consider the Nature and Qualifications, which are in the holy Scripture attributed to the Kingdom of Christ, and the Kingdom of Heaven here upon Earth. It is without question, that the Union of the Believers under Christ, their King, ought to be considered as a Kingdom or Empire, but such a one as is not of this World, and conse-

---

115. Acts 2:44, 45; 4:5.

quently of a quite different nature from that Sovereign Power, which is exercised in a Civil Government. Christ is there the King, who having withdrawn himself from our sight, has as it may be said, settled his Court in Heaven. His subjects are dispersed throughout all parts of the World, where the Christian Doctrine is taught and received by the Believers, who, by the intrinsick Vertue of this Doctrine, are confirmed in their Faith, and made proof against all the Temptations and Malice of this World. The Civil Power does not reach this Kingdom; true Piety being not to be implanted by Human Force, which is insufficient to procure God's Grace, or raise those inward Motions which are chiefly acceptable to God Almighty; and without which, all our exterior Actions, that may be enforced by a Civil Authority, are to be deem'd vain and fruitless. For, the Kingdom of Christ being a Kingdom of Truth, it requires no Civil Power or Force; For, Truth, by the help of the Christian Doctrine, and with the assistance of God's Grace, does gently insinuate it self into the Hearts of Men, and the Rewards or Punishments, which those are to receive, that either accept or despise this Doctrine, are reserved for the Life to come. He that will be pleased to examine those several Passages, where mention is made of the Kingdom of Christ, or the Kingdom of Heaven, may soon be convinced, that not any thing is to be met withal there, which has the least resemblance to a Civil Power or Sovereignty. Those that expect to enter into this Kingdom, must qualifie themselves by Repentance.[116] It is spoke of Christ himself, that he went about preaching the Gospel of the Kingdom of Heaven.[117] The Virtues and Qualifications which Christ requires in those, that will enter into his Kingdom, and consequently be blessed with eternal Salvation, have but little relation to the Qualifications of a Subject in a Civil Government. In that Kingdom every one is called great, or the least, according to his Proficiency in the Christian Doctrine, and according to his Obedience or disobedience to it.[118] We are commanded *first to seek the Righteousness of this King-*

---

116. Matt. 3:2, 4:17.
117. Matt. 4:23, 9:35.
118. Matt. 5:19, 7:21.

dom.[119] The great Mystery of this Kingdom is *the powerful operations of the Word of God.*[120] In this Kingdom are not only suffered those that are Foreigners to it, but also its Enemies, which is against the Maxims, of a Civil Government.[121] The Keys of this Kingdom are contained in the Doctrine of Remission of Sins.[122] And what is taught us concerning Precedency in the Kingdom of Heaven, is quite contrary to what is practised in a Civil *State.*[123] It is allowable by the Civil Constitutions, for every one to pursue his Right, but, in the Kingdom of Christ, he is counted an ill Subject, who will not remit a Trespass to his Brother.[124] The Kingdom of Christ is also of the little Children.[125] Those that are employed in this Kingdom have different Tasks, and undergo different sorts of Hardship, and yet their Reward is the same.[126] This Kingdom is taken from those that refuse it,[127] whereas it is a Maxim of Temporal Sovereigns, to force such as are refractory to Obedience; and this was the reason, why, after the Jews had despised it, it was offered to the Gentiles.[128] He that will enjoy the Benefit of this Kingdom must not be sloathful.[129] The richest find always the easiest Reception in a Civil State, but *the rich Man shall hardly enter into the Kingdom of Christ.*[130] He is accounted a good Subject in a State, who is industrious, and gathers Riches by all lawful ways and means; but this is reckoned as superfluous in the Kingdom of Heaven.[131] One of the chiefest Motives which induced Mankind to enter into Civil Societies, was, to preserve themselves and their Possessions; But Christ says: *Whoever he be of you,*

119. Matt. 6:33.
120. Matt. 13:21, 31, 33, 44, 45, 52.
121. Matt. 13:24, 47.
122. Matt. 16:19.
123. Matt. 18:1ff., 20:21ff., 23:8; Mark 9:33, 34; 10:42.
124. Matt. 18:23ff.
125. Matt. 19:14; Mark 10:14.
126. Matt. 20:1.
127. Matt. 21:43.
128. Matt. 22:2.
129. Matt. 25:1.
130. Matt. 19:23; Mark 10:23; Luke 12:33.
131. Luke 12:31.

that forsaked not all that he hath, he cannot be my Disciple.[132] And lastly of all, he says: *The Kingdom of God cometh not with observation; neither shall they say, lo here, or lo there, for behold, the Kingdom of God is within you.*[133] It would be superfluous to alledge more for the proof of it, all the rest being most of them the same in Substance.

§30. Though it be evident that, the Union of the Believers under Christ their King, and that Mystical Body, whose Head is Christ, the Members of all the Believers in general, cannot be considered as a Temporal State; nevertheless, it is worth our enquiry, whether not all those in General, that profess the Christian Doctrine, may be considered as a Body belonging under one Civil Government, or at least, have a near resemblance to a Civil Commonwealth? Or, which is the same in effect, Whether the Church, according to our Saviour's Intention ought to be considered as a State or Commonwealth? We take here the Word State, in its common Acceptation, *viz.* for a certain Society of Men, which being independent from any Foreign Jurisdiction, live under the Protection of their own Sovereigns. The main intention of this Question is, that, after we shall have made it appear, That the Church, according to the intention of Christ and his Apostles, neither was, nor could be a State, it may from thence be concluded, whether that Church which pretends to a Sovereignty, considered as such, be Christ's Church? But, to trace the very original of this Question, it ought first of all to be considered, in what Sense the Word *Ecclesia* or Church, is taken in the holy Scripture. The word *Ecclesia* has its off-spring out of the Democracy's of the *Greeks,* whereby they understood a Convention, Meeting, or sometimes, a Concourse of the People, or of a considerable Part of their Citizens, in order to receive Propositions, to consult and make Decrees, concerning Matters belonging to the Commonwealth. It is derived of *Evocare,* or to Call-forth, not, that thereby was always understood an Assembly, summoned out of a greater Multitude, (for I can see no reason why not all the Citizens had a Right to appear in

Whether the Church be a State?

What is understood in the holy Scripture by the word Ecclesia?

132. Luke 14:33.
133. Luke 17:20, 21.

those Assemblies;) but, because they were called out of their private Dwelling-places, and from their ordinary Business, to meet in a publick Place. So, that the original Signification of the Word, *Ecclesia,* implies not that of a State, but only a certain Qualification of a Democratical Government; it being evident, that a great number of Men cannot conveniently give their assent to a thing, unless they be Convened in one Place. In the Translation the *LXX* Interpreters, this Word is taken for a Convention, or Meeting of a considerable number of People; met, not only for the exercise of Divine Worship, but also for unlawful Ends.[134] So the *Greek* word ἐκκλησιάζειν, is taken for the Calling and Summoning an Assembly, about Matters concerning the Commonwealth.[135] But in the New Testament, the word *Ecclesia,* is, generally, taken, either, for all the Christians in General, wherever dispersed, or for the Congregation of the Believers in a certain Country, City, private House, or Family. In either sense, if we duely weigh the Attributes and Actions properly belonging to the Church (for by these we ought to judge of the Nature of a thing in Moral Cases) we do not meet with any thing, which has a relation to a Civil State. The true Encomium most frequently given to the Members of the Church is; that they are *Brothers, holy, and redeemed by the Blood of Christ.* Their chief Actions are said to be, *to hear the Word of God, to pray unto and praise God, to be Charitable, to walk in the fear of God, to Fast, and to provide for the Poor.* It is spoken of St. *Paul* and *Barnabas,* That they did Constitute Elders in those Churches, which they had planted in *Asia,*[136] where the word χειροτονήσαντες is made use of, which implies as much, as having made them by Suffrages of the Congregation; in the same manner as the Decrees used to pass in the antient Democracies, by the plurality of Votes; by which it appears, that they pretended to no Absolute Power of Constituting Elders over them, but such as were approved of by the Congregation. And it is remarkable that these, nevertheless are said to

What actions are celebrated in Scripture as belonging to the Church.

134. Ps. 26:5; Acts 19:32, 39, 40.
135. Num. 20:8, 10; Jos. 18:1, 2; Chron. 15:9, 10; 34:29.
136. Acts 14:23.

have been made *Overseers over the Church by the Holy Ghost.*[137] So were the Judges, that were set in the Land by *Jehosaphat, stiled Judges for the Lord;*[138] because, whoever is fitly qualified for any Office or Function, not contrary to the Word of God, and has obtained the same by lawful ways and Means, may justly be said to have been Constituted in that same Office by God Almighty. And though it belongs most properly to the Church to constitute Teachers, this nevertheless does not imply any Act of Sovereignty; it being evident, that a private Colledge or Society, subject to another Jurisdiction, may lawfully enjoy the same Power. A Dissension being arosen concerning an Article of Faith in the Church of *Antiocha,* they determined, that some of them should go concerning this Question then in dispute, to the Church of *Jerusalem;*[139] And these Deputies were by the rest of the Brethren, conducted out of the Town, in their way to *Jerusalem;* where this Question having been debated, and determined, they sent Word thus, to their Brethren, *It seemed good to the Holy Ghost, and us,* &c. where it is to be observed, that to send Deputies, concerning such Matters, as are not intended in prejudice of the Sovereign Power; for one Congregation to consult another, concerning any Articles of Faith; and to determine any Differences about them, are to be looked upon, as Actions of such a nature, which do not imply a Sovereign and Absolute Power; but may legally belong to a private Colledge, or sometimes a private Person; provided the Business in hand be not imposed upon its Members, but transacted and admitted by common consent. So the Church of *Jerusalem,* chose certain Men, who were to be Overseers of the Poor, which they had a Right to do, as being a Society or Colledge.[140] In the same Sense ought to be taken, what is said in the 2 Epistle to the *Corinthians, c.* 8:19. That the Churches had chosen one to travel with St. *Paul.* The Church is called *a Flock, which is to be fed by the Bishops,*

---

137. Acts 20:28.
138. 2 Chron. 19:5, 6.
139. Acts 15:2.
140. Acts 6:1ff.

with the pure Word of God, who are to preserve it from the Wolves; That is to say, from *Men speaking perverse things, to draw away Disciples after them;*[141] Against those Teachers the Church ought to be watchful, not ceasing to Admonish their Auditors to avoid their Snares. What concerns that passage in the 1 Epistle to the *Corinthians, c.* 6:1. and following *Verses,* it is apparent enough, that there is not any Sovereign Authority or Jurisdiction granted to the Christians, (barely considered as Christians:) But the Apostle enjoyns them, that in case of any Differences in Civil Affairs among the Members of the Church, they should rather refer it to the Arbitration of the Brethren, than to go to Law before the Gentiles, and fall under the Censure of being Avaricious. In the following Chapter, it is plainly expressed, that no body, by becoming a Member of the Church, does change his Qualification or Function, which belonged to him as a Subject; or that Christianity is inconsistent with the Subjection to a Civil Government;[142] a Servant therefore, by being a Christian, does not become a Freeman; neither is a Subject thereby absolved from the Allegiance due to his Sovereign;[143] concerning the Union and Modesty, which ought to be practised in the Church, or the Christian Congregations, where the Word of God was Preached, and the Sacraments Administred, St. *Paul* speaks in the 1 Epistle to the *Corinthians; c.* 11:18 and following *Verses;* and in the 14 *Chap.* 34:40 *Verse.* And, what sort of Religious Exercises was to be used in these Congregations, is expressed in the 1 Epistle to the *Corinthians, c.* 14. *viz.* to be *Hymns, Doctrines, Tongues, Prophesies, Revelations, Interpretations;* all which are to be applied to Edifie the Congregation; and in the 12 *Chapter,* 28 *Verse,* the several Degrees and Functions of the Members of the Church, are thus enumerated: First, *Apostles,* secondarily, *Prophets,* thirdly, *Teachers;* after that, *Miracles,* then *Gifts of Healings, Helps, Governments, Diversities of Tongues;*[144] All which are Requisites belonging to the propagating and establishing of

141. Acts 20:28, 29, 30.
142. Rom. 13:1.
143. 1 Tim. 6:1, 2.
144. Eph. 4:11.

the Gospel, and are Gifts of that self same Spirit, who dispenses his Gifts to every Man, as he pleases; So, that he, that has received more noble Endowments, can therefore not claim any Prerogative, as being a more honorable Member of this Mystical Body, or pretend to any Jurisdiction over such as are not endowed with these Qualifications in the same Degree as himself. And charity, which is the inseparable Attribute of all Christians, is more noble and excellent than all other spiritual Gifts.[145] Alms are the only Taxes which belong to the Church, and these also cannot be exacted by the Sovereign Authority of the Church;[146] Tho' it be undeniable; that every Church is obliged to maintain its Ministers. In the 2 Epist. to the *Corinthians, c.* 11:28. St. *Paul* professes, That *the Care of all the Churches lies upon him, to strengthen those that were weak, and to obviate Scandals.* And in the next following *Chapter,* he says, That the Church of *Corinth* is in no wise inferior to other Churches, which were planted by others, who had exercised the Apostolical Function before him.[147] Neither is any thing to be met withal in the Holy Scripture, which proves the Subordination of one Church to another; Nay, the Congregations of small Towns, and even of private Families, are often stiled Churches, as those of vast Cities; and those particular Churches, which were planted in *Judea,* are called the Churches of God.[148] In the Epistle to the *Ephesians, c.* 1:22. *c.* 5:23. and to the *Colossians, c.* 1:18, 24. Christ is called the *Head of the Body of the Church, which he has presented to himself a glorious Church, not having Spot or Wrinkle, or any such thing, but that it should be Holy and without Blemish, sanctified by Christ's Redemption, and cleansed with the washing of Water, by the Word.*[149] What Qualifications are required in a Bishop, or a Governour of a particular Church, is expressed in the 1 Epistle to *Timothy, c.* 3:2. and following *Verses;* in the 2 Epistle to *Timothy, c.* 4:2. in the Epistle to *Titus, c.* 1:7, 8, 9,

145. 1 Cor. 16:1; 2 Cor. 8:2, 3, 8; 1 Tim. 5:16.
146. Philipp. 4:15; 2 Cor. 9:14; 1 Tim. 5:18.
147. 2 Cor. 12:13. [Puf.]
148. 1 Thess. 2:14; 2 Thess. 1:4.
149. Ephes. 5:26, 27.

and *c.* 2:7. All which, if duely examined, have a relation meerly to the Purity of his Doctrine, and his being blameless in his Behaviour; and do not in the least favour of any thing properly belonging to the Supream Governours of a State. For, it is said, that he must be *the Husband of one Wife, Vigilant, Sober, of a good Behaviour, given to Hospitality, apt to Teach; Not given to Wine, no Striker, not greedy of Filthy Lucre; but patient, not a Bawler, not Covetous. One that ruled well his own House, having his Children in Subjection, with all Gravity; Not a Novice, not lifted up with Pride;* All which are such Vertues as belong properly to a Teacher, or a private Person, In the 1 Epistle to *Timothy, c.* 3:15. the Church is called, *the House of God;* σύλος καὶ ἑδραίωμα, or, *The Pillar and Ground of Truth;* like we are used to affix Proclamations to great Pillars, to the view of every body. Tho' some antient Manuscripts refer these words; *The Pillar and Ground of Truth,* to the following Sentence; the Preceding ending with the words, *The Church of the living God.* Then begins a new Sentence thus: *The pillar and ground of Truth, and without Controversy, great is the Mystery of Godliness, God was manifest in the Flesh,* &c. So, that, in this sense, this Passage is parallel to what Christ told St. *Peter* by St. *Matthew, c.* 16:18. and to that of St. *John, c.* 20:31. The Titles of Honour belonging to the Christian Church, are recited in the Epistle to the *Hebrews, c.* 12:22. where it is called, *The mount of Sion, the City of the living God, the heavenly Jerusalem, the innumerable Company of Angels; the General Assembly and Church of the first Born, which are written in Heaven, where God is the Judge of all, and Jesus the Mediator of the New Covenant, and the Spirit of just Men made perfect.*[150] And in the *Revelation, c.* 2:3. the Churches of *Asia* are praised for their good Deeds, and their Vices exposed, with a severe Commination, that, if they did not repent, their Candlestick (which is the Doctrine of the Gospel) should be taken away from them;[151] which is sufficient to shew, that the Light of the Gospel may be extinguished in particular *Churches.* All these passages, if duely compared and examined, do not furnish us with any Matter,

150. Hebr. 12:22, 23, 24. [Puf.]
151. Rev. 2:3, 5. [Puf.]

proving the Christian Church to be a State, or to have any resemblance to a Temporal Sovereignty.

§31. But; besides what has been said already, a great many Reasons may be alledged, which sufficiently prove, that it was not in the power of the Apostles, to plant a Church, resembling in Power, to a Temporal Sovereignty, if they had entertained any Thoughts of attempting a Design both unnecessary and illegal. The common Security is the main End of every Government, whereby Men are enabled to defend themselves by their united strength against all Injuries; which cannot be performed without a considerable number of stout and well appointed Men. But the Name of the Church, is often given to the Congregations of an indifferent Town, nay even of private Families; And does not our Saviour himself say? *Where two or three are gathered in my Name, there am I in the midst of them.*[152] Which moved *Tertullian* to say: *Three make up a Church, as well as a Colledge.*[153] And where Christ is in the midst of a Congregation, certainly there cannot be wanting sufficient Means to obtain Salvation, *viz.* the Word, the Minister, and the Sacraments; so, that the end and scope of the Christian Religion may be attained to, even in an indifferent numerous Congregation of the Believers. Neither does the greater number of the Believers joyned in one Church (like a vast number of People is necessary for the erecting of a State) in it self considered, add any thing, or is necessary for the obtaining the end of the Christian Religion, it being indifferent, in regard of obtaining Salvation; whether a Man worship God in a great or small Congregation. From whence this inference may be made, That, in case, the greatest part of the Church should separate itself from the others, the rest, notwithstanding all this, may pursue and obtain the End of the Christian Faith; Quite otherwise as it is with Temporal Commonwealths, where, if the greatest part of its Inhabitants happen to be rooted out, the rest will be thereby disinabled to maintain the State. These

The Condition of the primitive Church was such, as not to permit a Sovereignty within it self.

---

152. Matt. 18:20.
153. Quintus Septimus Florens Tertullian, *On Exhortation to Chastity* (*De exhortatione castitatis*), chap. 7. [SZu]

Qualifications belonging to Subjects; especially to such of them as are to be preferred before others in a State, either for their Usefulness, or the honour of the Commonwealth are not esteemed the same in the Church, so, that he, who does not excel in Riches, Strength or Wisdom, shall therefore not be deemed a good Christian.[154] Furthermore; those that pretend to lay the Foundation of a new State, must have Territories belonging to them, where their new Subjects may settle themselves and their Fortunes. And, all such as live, or are seated in a Commonwealth, if they pretend to set up a new State, must either transplant themselves into another Country, or else overturn that Government, under which they then live. So, when *Moses* delivered the *Israelites* from the *Aegyptian* Bondage, he led them into the Desarts of *Arabia*. And, when *Romulus* had resolved to erect a new Commonwealth, he first withdrew himself from the Subjection of the Kings of *Alba;* and such of the Neighbouring Countries, as were for being Members of that new Commonwealth, did leave their former Habitations, and settled themselves in *Rome.* But neither Christ, nor his Apostles, did ever remove Christians from their Habitations to other Places, but allowed every body to remain in the same Station, and under the same Government, without the least prejudice to the former Rights of their Sovereigns over them. From whence it is evident, that the Christians, tho' never so numerous, could not be in a condition to settle themselves under any one State of their own. For, since, according to the Rules of the Christian Religion, the Rights of Sovereigns over their Subjects Lives and Goods, are not taken away or impair'd, and no body can be subject to two Masters, there could be no pretence of erecting a new Sovereignty; especially in the midst of another Commonwealth, nay, it was beyond their Power, even to enter into such a Society, as should be in the least prejudicial to the Rights of their present Sovereigns.[155] Who can be so ignorant in civil Affairs, as not to understand, what prodigious Sums of Money are required for the maintaining of a State. And, tho' the Rights of Sovereigns do not extend so far as to take away from Subjects the

154. 1 Cor. 1:20, 21, 22.
155. Rom. 13:1ff.; Pet. 2:13.

private disposal of their Goods; nevertheless may they lawfully restrain the Extravagancy of their Subjects, if they pretend to dispose of their Goods in prejudice of the State. For; if this Liberty should be granted to the Subjects without limitation, the State, if deprived of its nourishment would quickly be reduced to a languishing condition, or else, private Men might be enabled to erect a new State in the midst of the old one, or at least, to impair, and endanger the Publick Safety. And, since those Sovereigns, under whose Jurisdiction the Apostles lived, had the same Right over the Fortunes of their Subjects, as other Governments have; and the Rights of Sovereigns were not taken away, by the Doctrine of Christ, there could be no other provision made for the maintainance of those Congregations, (as such) but what was consistent with the lawful Rights of their Sovereigns, and as much only as might lawfully be given by private Persons; which could not exceed a private Fortune, and were nothing more than Voluntary Contributions or Alms; And, whatsoever of any real Estate was attributed to these Uses, was thereby not exempted from paying of Taxes, no more than the Estates of other Subjects.

§32. But if we take a full view of the whole Structure of Civil Societies, and by what means Subjects were united under one Government; we shall find them to differ as Heaven and Earth from that Union, which belongs properly to the Body of a Church. If we trace that Original of Civil Societies or Commonwealths, it is evident, that Men having found the Inconveniencies and Dangers which attended a solitary Life in the free natural State, did enter and unite themselves into Societies for their common Security: And having agreed to a certain Form of Government, did constitute one certain Person, or a Counsel, who were to be the supream Governours of that Society; unto whom they submitted themselves and their fortunes, for the common Benefit of that Society. But Churches were erected upon quite another Foundation. For here, Men, being made sensible of their miserable condition, did not by their own accord and a general agreement, turn themselves to God Almighty, but, being on the contrary overwhelmed with Darkness and Ignorance, so, as to be over secure, and neglecting their own

The inward Structure of the Church is quite different from that of a State.

Salvation, God did send his Messengers among them, *commanding all men every where to repent.*[156] Here is not the least footstep of any general Agreement of Men to erect and submit themselves under one Church; but each particular Person for himself, without any respect or regard to others did follow Christ and his Doctrine. And, whereas in a Civil State, the whole family has its dependency from their Master, and enjoys all the Privileges belonging to them under his Protection; it is quite different in the Church, where the Wife is not obliged to follow her Husband's Religion, nor the Servant the Master.[157] So, were in the family of *Narcissus* (who himself was not a Christian) several Christian Servants, who are saluted as such by S. *Paul.*[158] And in this sense is to be taken what is said by Christ, He that loved Father or Mother, Son or Daughter, more than me, is not worthy of me.[159] As likewise what is mentioned concerning Divisions, Discords, Dissensions, which are to be raised by the Doctrine of Christ among the nearest Friends, is to be understood of the strict Union betwixt Christ and the Believers, which surpasses, and is to be preferred before all the Tyes of Consanguinity among Men.[160] So that, if a Father, Husband or Master, should turn Apostate, the Son, Wife or Servant are not obliged to follow their footsteps. Neither is it requisite to be solicitous about any particular or certain Form of Government in the Church, *viz.* whether the same ought to be Monarchical, Aristocratical or Democratical. For, these several Forms belonging only to a Civil Government are very preposterously made use of in the behalf of the Church, which is far different from a Temporal State. And as Churches and Commonwealths are erected for different Ends: so the Offices belonging to both are altogether of a different Nature. Who is so ignorant as not to know, that for the obtaining the Ends of Civil Societies, it was requisite to constitute various Degrees of Dignities appertaining to the Managers of

156. Acts 17:30.
157. 1 Cor. 7:12.
158. Rom. 16:11.
159. Matt. 10:37, 12:50; Luke 14:26.
160. Matt. 10:34. (Luke 12:51. [Puf.])

the State; whereas the most plain and natural Distinction betwixt Christians in reference to the Church, is only that of Teachers and Auditors.

§33. Besides all this, the Teachers in a Church, do not only differ from Temporal Governours in a State, in that these are constituted for different Ends: But the main Difference is the very nature of their Constitution. We will not insist here upon the Point of Succession, by which a great many Sovereigns obtain their Sovereign Power, which is quite otherwise in the Church: But we will only treat in this place concerning the different Constitution betwixt Teachers, and such Sovereigns, as exercise the Supream Civil Power, by Vertue of Election. When therefore the Sovereign Power is lodged in any Persons by Election, the rest who have thus chosen them their Supream Governour, do thereby submit themselves to the Disposal of those their Sovereigns, in such a manner as to oblige themselves, that whatsoever they think conducing for the publick Welfare, shall be taken as such by the whole Body; and that they will always be ready to execute their Commands: Wherefore Sovereigns are always invested with a full Power to force their Subjects to a compliance with their Commands, by inflicting Punishments upon them. But how is it possible to imagine that any Church or Congregation of the Believers should ever, or ought to submit themselves so entirely to the Pleasure and Disposal of their Teachers; as to oblige themselves to acquiesce barely in, and to follow blindly, whatever shall be proposed by them, as conducing and leading to the way of Salvation; it being certain without contradiction, that none of the Believers do entirely submit themselves and their Faith to any Body but to God Almighty, whose Will and Commands ought to be interpreted by the Teachers of the Church, and their Auditors to be exhorted to a due Compliance with them. For, whoever it be, that proposes any Doctrine surpassing human Reason, if he pretends to gain credit by his Auditors, must either claim it by Vertue of his own Authority, or by Compulsion, or by Vertue of a more Superiour Power. But any Man that offers Matters not agreeable to Reason, does thereby expose himself, and so looses his Authority, except he can by other more powerful

There is a great difference betwixt Teachers in a Church, and the Governours of a State.

means maintain his Doctrine, and gain credit with his Auditors. It was for this Reason, that, to the Greeks, who were Men that sought after Wisdom and Reason, the Preaching of the Apostles was Foolishness.[161] And *S. Paul* was for the same Reason nick-named a *Babler* by the *Athenian* Philosophers.[162] Neither is any human Power capable of enforcing the Mysteries of Faith and the Christian Doctrine upon People; for which reason Christ told his Apostles, Go and Teach, and Believe, and that with all your hearts; to obtain which, all human means which imply any Temporal Advantages, or are forcible in their own nature, are to be taken for Trifles and insufficient. There is then no other Way left, but that such Doctrines must be verified by a Superiour Being or Principle, *viz.* the Grace of God, which always accompanies the Gospel, and those Miracles wherewith the Apostles antiently authorized their Doctrine;[163] Tho' it is at the same time undeniable, that since the Gospel is sufficiently spread abroad in the World, we do not now any more stand in need of such Miracles: In the same manner as the Thunder and Lightning which were heard at the Publishing of the Ten Commandments, were never repeated afterwards among the *Jews.* The Christians therefore have submitted their Faith and Reason only to Christ, whose Authority is unquestionable, as being God himself, and was testified by his Father's Voice from Heaven, when he said, *This is my beloved Son, in whom I am well pleased.*[164] And, as the People of *Israel* willingly submitted their Faith to *Moses,* as soon as he had given them plain Demonstrations of his Divine Commission;[165] so were they obliged to submit their Faith to the Apostles, after they had once verified their Divine Commission by their Miracles: Tho' it cannot be denied, but that their Doctrine did sometimes produce good Effects without Miracles. It is therefore very observable, that when they preached and taught their Doctrine to such as were well versed in the

---

161. 1 Cor. 1:23.
162. Acts 17:18.
163. Mark 16:20; Acts 14:3; Hebr. 2:4.
164. Matt. 3:17; Luke 3:22.
165. Exod. 20:19.

Old Testament, they did not take it amiss, if their Auditors examined their Words, whether they were consonant with the Prophesies contained therein.[166] From whence it is sufficently apparent, that no body ought to engage himself unto a blind Obedience of such Teachers, as cannot verifie their immediate Divine Commission by Miracles, so as to make his Faith absolutely dependant from their Doctrine without Exception, but only so far, as their Doctrine is found agreeable to the Doctrine of those who had given manifest demonstrations of their divine Authority. And for this Reason it is, that it is not sufficient for a Teacher in the Church to say, so it is, and so it shall and must be: But he lies under an indispensible Obligation of making it plain and apparent, that, what he offers to his Auditors, is absolutely consonant to the Doctrine published by Christ and his Apostles. Neither ought the Auditors pin their Faith upon the Authority of their Teachers, but to refer themselves to the Authority of God and his Word, which is the Touchstone by which the Teachers Doctrine is to be examined and approved. The Schools of Philosophers used to take their Names from their Chief Teachers or Founders, as we may observe in the Schools of *Plato, Aristoteles* and *Zeno:* But the Church ought to have no other Name, but that she is the Church of God or Christ. It was upon that score when S. *Paul* rebuked the *Corinthians,* because some of them said, they were of *Paul,* some of *Apollo,* some of *Cephas,* and some of *Christ.*[167] So that since the holy Scripture is now established among us, Christians ought not to be like the Disciples of *Pythagoras,* who used for their Motto, that old Saying αὐτὸς ἔφα, *He himself has spoken it:*[168] But they have sufficient Authority to look themselves into the Holy Scripture, and to examine whether the Doctrine of their Teachers be agreeable to the Doctrine of our Saviour. For, Christ, when he said, *search the Scriptures,* did not only speak to his Disciples, but to his

166. Acts 17:11.
167. 1 Cor. 1:12.
168. In the middle of the fifth century B.C., the order of the Pythagoreans split into two parties. Whereas one group (that used the motto quoted by Pufendorf) did not wish to depart from Pythagoras's own words, the other one deemed it more appropriate to develop his teachings by reflection. [SZu]

Auditors in general. And *S. Paul* bid us *to prove all things, and to hold fast that which is good.*[169] *S. John* says, *that we shall try the Spirits, whether they are of God.*[170] Neither can I conceive how the Examination of our selves, which *S. Paul* so highly recommends to all that intend to be Partakers of the Lords Supper, can be duely performed without meditating the Scriptures.[171] For, in this case, I take the condition of a Teacher and of a Physician, to be quite different; it being only required in the latter to understand the Art of Physick, and to apply the same to his Patients, which may be done with good Success, tho' they be never so ignorant. But it is not sufficient for a Teacher of a Church to be alone versed in the Articles of the Christian Religion; that Church being to be deemed most excellent, where the Auditors are not inferiour to their Teachers in the Cognition of the Mysteries of the Faith. For the Apostles did not shun to declare unto Mankind all the Counsel of God,[172] having not committed the Christian Doctrine to the care and custody of one particular Person, who was to be the only Interpreter of it, as the Sibyllin Oracles were antiently at *Rome* in the Custody of the *Decemviri.*[173] And because Christians do not build their Faith upon any Human Authority, but upon the Word of God alone, they are said to be taught of God.[174] For which Reason *S. Paul* utterly denied that they had any Dominion over the Faith of the *Corinthians;* or, which is the same in effect, that they could exercise any Dominion over them under the Pretence of Faith.[175] For the rest, as Christians which are well versed in the Scriptures, may, without great difficulty, try their Teacher's Doctrine by the Touchstone of the Holy Scripture: So the Catechism and other compendious Instructions relating to the chiefest Articles of the Christian Faith may be sufficient for those of a meaner Capacity, wherein all Christians ought to be well instructed in their

169. John 5:39; 1 Thess. 5:21.
170. 1 John 4:1.
171. 1 Cor. 11:28.
172. Acts 20:27.
173. See note 78, above. [SZu]
174. John 6:45; 1 Thess. 4:9.
175. 2 Cor. 1:24.

younger Years, both by their Parents and Teachers of the Church, this being likely to prove more useful to those of an indifferent Capacity than all the other Subtilities and Controversies, which in themselves are not absolutely necessary, or requisite to be understood by every Christian in particular. And if we duely consider what is required by the Apostle for the obtaining of Salvation, we shall find that this Knowledge may be attained to without much Difficulty; because the Confession that *Jesus was Christ, the Son of God,* is the Foundation Stone, and, as it was, the Center of the Christian Religion,[176] and that this Article was chiefly opposed by the Gates of Hell in the time of the Primitive Christians, the Apostle S. *John* prescribes this as a general Rule to be particularly taken notice of by such as are of a mean Capacity: *Hereby know you* (said he) *the Spirit of God: Every Spirit that confesseth, that Jesus Christ is come in the Flesh, is of God; and every Spirit that confesseth not, that Jesus Christ is come in the Flesh, is not of God.*[177] Though from hence no Inference ought to be made, as if Christians may neglect, or ought not also to be well instructed concerning all the other Articles of Faith, or that it is indifferent for any Christian to believe, what he pleases, concerning the rest of the Articles of the Christian Doctrine.

§34. It being then evident, that there is a great difference betwixt the condition of particular Churches, and that of a State or Commonwealth: It may further be enquired into, whether perhaps those Churches united don't make up a Body like to that of a great State? For it is certain, that the Word Church is in the Scriptures attributed to the whole Body of the Believers wheresoever dispersed throughout the World; yet so, that there is not the least appearance (if a due regard be had to our Saviour's Intention) of a Design to erect a State. *Go you into all the World, and Preach the Gospel to every Creature,* are the Words of our Saviour to his Disciples.[178] Here is no mention made of any

Whether the whole Christian Church ought to be considered as a State.

176. Rom. 10:9, 10; 1 Tim. 1:5; 2 Tim. 2:22; John 20:31.
177. 1 John 4:2, 3.
178. Mark 16:15.

Persons, who should be the supream Governours over the rest (as is usual, and absolutely necessary in a State) nor any certain Place of Residence appointed for these Governours, from whence the rest should receive their Orders. Neither is the least care taken by what means they should maintain a Correspondency with their capital City: And truly, considering the vast Extent of the World, and the prodigious Distance of those Countries, where the Apostles Preach'd the Gospel: (besides, that there was a mortal Enmity betwixt some of these States) these were unsurmountable Obstacles for the settling and maintaining a Correspondency betwixt them. So that it does not appear, by what means all the Christians could be united under one State. It is not denied but that there is often mention made in the Scripture, of the Union of the Christians; as in the 1 *Cor. c.* 12:12, 13. *As the body is one, and had many members, and all the members of that one body being many, are one body: So also is Christ. For by one Spirit are we all baptized into one body, whether we be Jews or Gentiles, whether we be bond or free, and have been all made to drink into one Spirit.* Christ says in the 10. Chap. of *S. John,* ver. 16, *My Sheep hear my voice, and there shall be one fold and one shepherd.* Which shews, that all the Sheep are brought into one Flock by hearing the Voice of their Pastour, who is Christ. So it is said in the Epistle to the *Ephesians,* ch. 4: ver. 2, 3, 4, 5, 6, *Forbearing one another in love, endeavouring the Unity of the Spirit in the bond of peace. There is one body and one Spirit, even as you are called in one hope of your calling: One Lord, one Faith, one Baptism, one God and Father of all.* And Christ, in his farewel Sermon, does chiefly recommend to his Disciples Charity and Unity, as the true Badges of Christianity; And the Name of Brother which particularly belongs to the Christians, seems to imply a general union betwixt them.[179] But if we consider the Nature of these holy Tyes, we may easily observe them to have been in no ways adapted to the Constitution of a temporal Government; but properly belonging to the Establishment and Union of a mystical Body. For, as none of them requires or implies any dependency from

179. John 13:34; 1 Cor. 13; Coloss. 3:14; Gal. 6:10.

a Temporal Power, so they may belong in common to all Christians, tho' living in far distant Countries, and several Jurisdictions.

§35. Neither does it appear, for what end or purpose all the Christians in General should be reduced under one State. For, each Congregation or Church may with more ease and conveniency constitute Teachers in their Churches, fitly qualified for the Ministry of the Gospel, and have a more watchful Eye over those who are known, and near at hand, than can be expected from one single Person, (tho' never so wise) living at a great distance; who being besides this, overwhelmed with multitude of Businesses, is forced to see with other Peoples Eyes, and to hear with other Peoples Ears. Neither is it a sufficient Reason, what is alledged, that for the composing and determining of such Differences as may arise betwixt the Teachers of the Church, or betwixt them and others, a General Court ought to be established in the Christian Church, it being evident, that such Cases can be no where determined with more conveniency, than in the same Government where they live; and that there cannot any sufficient reason be given, why they should not acknowledge the same Jurisdiction with the rest of their fellow Subjects. There is one objection which has something of colour in it; for it is alledged, That if all the Christian Churches throughout the World were united under one Head, (whether under one Person, or a certain Assembly, matters not) the unity of Faith might be better preserved, Controversies sooner composed, and Heresies suppressed or quite extinguished; but if the whole matter be duely weighed, it will appear, that such an Ecclesiastical Monarch may be very easily spared in the Church. For, granting such an universal Judge of all Controversies arising in the Church, he must be supposed to be infallible, (and that beyond all contradiction) as well in point of Matter of Fact, as to the lawfulness of the Case; for it may so happen, that it be plain enough, whether a Doctrine be erroneous or not, when at the same time, it may be disputable, whether the said Error ought to be laid to a certain Man's Charge or not? For, if an Appeal be allowed from this Judge, after Sentence pronounced, there will never be an end of the Process. It is therefore absolutely requisite, that this infallible Authority

There is no necessity for Christians to be united under one State.

Whether it be necessary to set up a general Judge of all Controversies in the Church?

should be so manifestly proved, that it cannot reasonably be called in question. For, unless this Authority be unquestionable for the decision of this Controversie, we must run from this Judge to another, who must also be supposed to be Infallible, and so in infinite; it being granted by all, without Exception, that no body ought to be a Judge in his own Case. And, since this Privilege of being Infallible, could not be granted by any body, but by God alone; (the whole Body of Christians, being not invested with such a Power) it must plainly be proved out of the Scriptures, that this particular Prerogative and Authority was granted to one certain Person, for him and his Successors to decide all Controversies concerning the Articles of Faith, without being liable to any Error. But, of this there is not the least footstep in the holy Scripture; Nay, the Apostles, when they were sent by Christ into all the World, were endued with the same Spirit, and had an equal Authority. So, that there is but one way now left, for the attaining to the true Knowledge of the Christian Religion, both for the Teachers in the Church, and all Believers in general, which is, to study the Scriptures devoutly, and without Intermission.[180] And whoever pretends to Inspiration, or to a prophetical Spirit, ought by undeniable Demonstrations to justifie his Pretensions. These Qualifications, which the Apostle *Paul* describes in the 2 Epistle to *Timothy, c.* 2:24, 25, ought to be applied to all Bishops and Teachers in general: *And the Servant of the Lord,* he says, *must not strive, but be gentle unto all Men, apt to teach patiently. In meekness instructing those that oppose themselves, if God peradventure will give them Repentance to the acknowledging of the Truth.* Out of what has been said, it is apparent, that, if any one now a-days, does pretend to any Prerogative, or Infallibility in deciding Controversies as to matter of Faith, he ought to be endued with such extraordinary Qualifications, as are most requisite for the due Explaining and Interpreting the Sense of the holy Scripture, and this in so high a degree, as that the other Teachers in the Church are not able to stand in Competition with him, nay, that even all their joint Endeavours, in

180. 2 Tim. 3:14, 15.

this kind, are not to be compared to his Judgment. Besides this, it must be supposed, that this universal Judge (except he be to be look'd upon as an useless Engine) must be invested with a Power to execute his Decrees, and to oblige all Christians to acquiesce in his Judgment; For, if it be supposed, that his Decrees have no other force, than as far as they influence People by the force of Truth, they would be either useless, or else this Judge in vain pretends thereby to any further Prerogative, but what he has in common with other Christians that apply themselves to the Study of the holy Scripture. Furthermore, this obliging Power must either have been obtained by a peculiar Privilegde granted by God Almighty, or by a general consent of the Christians, or by an inherent Right to a Sovereignty over all the Christian Churches. As for a priviledge granted by God, or the general consent of the Christian Churches, there is not the least Proof of it, as far as ever I could find; And as to the pretended Sovereign Power, its legal Title ought to be proved by such Documents as are suitable to so great a Pretension. For it is a very insignificant Proof, to alledge in a case of such Moment Tradition, and a long continued Usurpation, which adds nothing to the right of a long continued illegal Possession, and cannot be taken for a solid Foundation, whereupon to build a real Pretension to such a Sovereignty; for it is possible, that, whereas something of a Prerogative was intended in the primitive times, the same, in process of Time, has been abused, and consequently degenerated into an insufferable Tyranny. We cannot therefore, but look upon such a Tradition, as has not the least foundation in the Scriptures, as very suspicious; especially, when we consider, that such a Sovereign Power is quite contrary to the true Genius of the Christian Religion. It may perhaps be objected, that nothing else can be so powerful to put a stop to all Controversies; but it ought to be considered also, that thereby the worsest sort of Slavery must be introduced, worse than that whereof *Tacitus* complains in his time: *Adempto, per Inquisitiones, & loquendi audiendiq; Commercio, atque ipsacum voce memoria perdatur, si tam in nostra potestate foret oblivisci, quam tacere. By the Inquisition the benefit of our Tongue and Ears is taken away at once; and if it was as easie to controul Mens Memories, as it is to bridle their Tongues, the very remem-*

brance of things past, had been long ago abolished among us.[181] Truly, by
such Methods, perhaps the Commonwealth may be stock'd with Hypocrites, and dissembling Hereticks, but few will be brought over to the
Orthodox Christian Faith. As it is therefore absolutely requisite, that
a hidden Ulcer should be laid open, whereby it may the sooner be
purg'd from its Malignancy, and proper Remedies more immediately
be applied to the affected Part; So, is it much conducing in the Church,
that such Scruples and Erroneous Opinions as have seised our Minds
should be brought to light, that by applying timely Remedies, they
may be removed before they are gone too far; than by couching them
over to let them run into a malignant Suppuration, which at last may
turn to an incurable Gangren. It is also to be taken notice of, that if
this Ecclesiastical Sovereignty be granted, there must of necessity be a
double headed Sovereign Power in one State; it being evident, that
Subjects would be obliged to acknowledge the Authority of this Ecclesiastical Judge in point of Controversie, as well, and in the same measure, as they do the Authority of their civil Governours in civil Actions. And, since this Ecclesiastical Sovereignty has a different scope
from that, for which Civil Societies were erected, it must consequently
be of a quite different nature, and make up a particular Sovereignty.
Wherefore, if both these should happen to be joined in one person, he
becomes thereby at once master over our Lives and Consciences: But,
if this Ecclesiastical Jurisdiction be lodged in another Person, he must
either at the same time be acknowledged to have a Power of executing
his Decrees, by his own Prerogative, or else to have only an Authority
of giving Sentence, leaving the Execution of it to the civil Magistrates.
If the first of these two be supposed, it is evident, that a double headed
Sovereignty must carry along with it great Inconveniencies and Dis-
tractions; and if the latter, those that exercise the Sovereignty in the
State, must be look'd upon as Executioners only to this holy Judge.
All these Things duely considered, as they must needs occasion great
Convulsions in the State, so no man that is not beyond his Wits will

---

181. P. Cornelius Tacitus, *The Life of Gnaeus Julius Agricola,* chap. 2. [SZu]

be apt to imagine, (unless it be made appear by most evident Proofs)
that Christ intended to introduce, by his Doctrine, such pernicious
Diseases into civil Societies. For, tho' it is impossible, that no Controversies should be raised in the Church, like Christ himself has foretold
it in the Parable by *Matthew, c.* 13:24. And St. *Paul* in the 1 Epistle to
the *Corinthians, c.* 11:19. Nevertheless, if any Controversie does arise,
he that is the first Author of it must of necessity maintain his Opinion,
under a colour at least of its being agreeable to the Scriptures. For, if
any one should pretend to introduce a new Article of Faith, without
endeavouring to prove it out of the holy Scripture, he would be look'd
upon as a mad Man, tho' he should call to his aid all the Sophistications
of the Philosophers. And if he should insist upon the Authority of
Traditions without the Scriptures, this would only serve to disclose the
weakness of that Foundation whereupon he builds his Doctrine. But,
if any one should make an attempt against any Article of Faith, received
already as such, in the Church, he is scarce worth taking notice of,
unless he should be able to alledge at least, some specious Reasons out
of the holy Scripture for his Opinion. And, in such a case (especially
if his Endeavours seem to proceed from a real Love to Truth) he ought
not to be absolutely slighted, without being heard, and his Reasons
examined. So, that then the whole decision of the Matter must depend
from a right Interpretation of the several passages in the holy Scripture
relating to this Controversie; And to find out this Interpretation, I see
not any necessity, which obliges us to have recourse to a Sovereign
Power, or any infallible Authority, but only to such Means, as are most
proper for the searching into, and finding out the genuine Sense of
other Authors; *viz.* by a true Knowledge of the Tongue, and a diligent
search into the nature and whole frame of the Christian Religion, and
by duely comparing the Articles of Faith, and observing their Analogy
and Connexion; Whosoever besides this, has a natural good Judgment,
and is not prepossessed with Prejudice, private Interest, or Passion, it
will be no such difficult Task for him, to find out the genuine Sense
of the Scriptures, and to demonstrate it so plainly, that such as oppose
him, will, by the consent of all Understanding People, be judged to be
in the wrong. So did our Saviour at several times convince the Pharisees

and Saduceans out of the whole Scripture, and by the force of his Arguments taken from thence, that they were not able to make any further reply. And why should it not be reasonably supposed, that in each Christian Church, there may be found a sufficient number of Teachers, capable of disproving such as pretend to introduce among them Innovations, and false Doctrines. But, supposing that these alone should prove insufficient, they may call to their aid those of the Neighbouring most famous Churches. From whence it appears, that there is no absolute Necessity of acknowledging a Judge General of Controversies in the Church. And, put the Case, that those that dissent from the Church, are so numerous, as to have spread their Doctrine all over the State, this Judge will prove useless in his Offices; For, if he pretends to have recourse to violent means to make them renounce their false Opinion, they will in all probability oppose force to force; But, if he takes the other way, and endeavours to convince them of their Error by Arguments taken out of the holy Scripture; this may be done as well by other Teachers fitly qualified for their Office; than by such a Judge General in the Church. Neither ought we to be so over timerous as to believe, that Errors should in so much prevail over Truth, as to domineer always and every where over it, it being not to be question'd, but that by help of the most clear-sighted Teachers in the Church, these Clouds may be soon dispersed, and Truth again appear in its splendor. I appeal to Experience, whether not a great many Heresies by the only help of prevailing Truth, without the assistance of such a Judge, or any human Force have by degrees dwindled away, and at last quite disappeared. It must be confest, there are some erroneous Opinions, which being nourished and maintained by a Temporal Interest, and certain Reasons of State of some particular Churches, are not so easie to be suppressed. Of this kind are those Controversies, wherein the Protestants differ with the Papishes; All which, if duely considered, are so deeply entangled with the Interest of the Popish Monarchy, that it is impossible for the *Roman Catholicks* to recede an Inch from the point of the controverted Articles, without diminution of their Authority, and endangering their great Revenues; so, that all hopes of an Union betwixt them and the *Protestants,* are in vain, unless the latter can resolve to submit themselves under the same Popish Yoak which they have shaken off so long ago. I cannot sufficiently admire that gross way of Arguing, made use of by the Papishes, when they talk of nothing else but the Authority of their Church, telling us, that, if we would but once acknowledge the same, all the Differences and Questions concerning the chief Articles of Faith would fall-a-course, making themselves both Party and Judge, and pretending to give Sentence in their own Case according to their own Testimony. They always make use of this Sophism, that they attribute only to themselves the glorious Name of the *True Church,* excluding all other Christians from it, but such as are of the same Communion with them. And, to back this pretence, nothing is more common among them, than to lay aside all manner of demonstrative Arguments founded in the Scriptures, and in lieu thereof, to find out new Methods (unknown to the Apostles) of Converting People; and to endeavour to establish their Authority by all manner of violence against those, that dare to maintain Truth in opposition to their Doctrine. For which reason God has threatned in a most peculiar manner to destroy this Monster of a State.[182]

§37. The true Method of composing Controversies arisen in the Church, is taught us by what is set us as an Example of this kind in the *Acts, c.* 15. where it deserves our most particular Observation, that the Controversy then in question was concerning a main Point in the Christian Religion, *viz.* Whether a man might be saved without being circumcised according to the Institution of *Moses.* For S. *Paul,* in the Epistle to the *Galatians, c.* 5:2. had positively declared: *If you be circumcised, Christ shall profit you nothing.* And it is very remarkable, that this Question was started in the very Infancy of the Church, when the Canon of the Church was not perfected, and there were not wanting living Testimonies of such as had received the Doctrine of Christ from his own mouth, and were endued with the Holy Ghost, and instructed with an Apostolical Authority. Neither is it to be doubted, but that

An Example of Controversie composed in the times of the Apostles.

182. For unknown reasons, in the Latin edition section 36 has been included in section 35. The translator obviously followed the original. [SZu]

Paul and *Barnabas* were endued with a sufficient Share of Wisdom and Understanding of the Holy Scripture, for the reducing of this Errour; as plainly appears out of the 5. verse of the above alledged Chapter,[183] that they opposed such forcible Reasons against this erroneous Opinion, that those that were come thither out of *Judea,* were not able to contradict them: So they appealed to the Authority of the Church of *Jerusalem,* which being the Spring from whence the Christian Religion was derived into other Parts of the World, they hoped to be back'd in this Opinion by such of the Members of that Church, as did not without some Reluctancy brook the Abolishing of the *Jewish* Synagogue; and that they were not quite beyond their guess, but met with a great many there that were addicted to the same Opinion, appears out of the 5th Verse in the same 15th Chapter. To prevent therefore any further Disturbance, which might be raised in the *Antiochian* Church by reason of this Controversie, *Paul* and *Barnabas,* with some others, were deputed to go to the Church of *Jerusalem,* to decide this Controversie. When they came thither a Convocation was called, consisting not only of the Apostles and Presbyters, but also of the other Members of that Church, not excepting those of the contrary side: After their Reasons had been heard, the Case was in debate a considerable time; and at last the whole matter having been sufficiently disputed on both sides, then *Peter* rose up, not as an universal Judge, or who pretended to decide the Controversie by Virtue of his Authority, but his Proceeding was by demonstrative Arguments, telling them, what prodigious Effects had been wrought among the Gentiles by his preaching the Gospel to them, after the Vision which appeared to him at *Joppe;*[184] Where he thus argues: That since the Holy Ghost had in the same measure purified the Hearts of those Believers that were uncircumcised, it would be unreasonable to put this Yoak upon the Neck of the Christians, the more, because they were not to be saved by Circumcision, but through the Grace of the Lord Jesus Christ. *Paul* and *Barnabas,* being of the same Opinion, did declare at the same time what Miracles

183. Acts 15:2.
184. Acts 11:4ff.

and Wonders God had wrought among the Gentiles by them, which
would not have been done, if they were to be taken for unsanctified,
as being not circumcised, or if Circumcision was an essential Part of
the Christian Faith. After all had held their Peace, that is to say, no
body further appearing who could contradict them or oppose their
Arguments, *James* at last arose, declaring that the Vision of *Peter* did
agree to the Words of the Prophets, and that therefore it was his Opinion that such among the Gentiles as did turn to Christ ought not to
be troubled. But that they also in some measure might gratifie themselves, and to induce them not to fly the Conversation of such of the
Gentiles as received the Christian Faith, it was thought fit that these
should abstain from Pollution of Idols, from Fornication, from things
strangled, and from Blood, all which was forbidden by the *Mosaic* Law,
and partly disagreeable to the Law of Nature; as Fornication, which
nevertheless was a common Vice among the Gentiles; the rest being
things indifferent in themselves, might easily be let alone, rather than
give Offence to a Brother. This having been approved of by common
Consent, and as it appears, even by those that were of a contrary Sen-
timent before, a Synodical Epistle was writ to the Church at *Antioch,*
in the name not only of those Apostles and Elders, but also of the
Brethren of the Church of *Jerusalem. Judas* and *Silas* were deputed to
carry this Epistle, who being arrived at *Antioch,* did not publish it in
the nature of a Law, but, having delivered it to the Brethren, (from
whom it met with a general Approbation) they exhorted them with
many words to a due Observance of it.

§38. If the whole matter be duly weighed, it furnishes us with several
Observations, which may not a little contribute towards the Explaining
the Nature of Ecclesiastical Councils. In the first place, it is most apparent, that these Councils are not such Bodies whose Authority is
everlasting for the Government of the Church: But that they are extraordinary Convocations or Conventions, composed out of some selected and most eminent Men of the Church, who are called together
for the composing certain Controversies arisen in the Church. And,
because those Councils were very frequent in the Church from its

Some
Observations
concerning
the nature
and use of
Councils.

Primitive times, this alone may serve as a convincing Argument, that the Church never acknowledged one infallible Judge for the deciding of Controversies. For to what purpose were so many Heads set to work, if one single Person was sufficient and infallible in the Decision of them? And (what is yet more) if the Decrees of the Councils had only their obliging Force from his Confirmation. Furthermore, those that compose such a Council are not to be considered as Members of an Assembly or Colledge, who by the Majority of Votes can so absolutely determine the Question in hand, as to be obligatory to all Christians in general; Truth generally speaking, not depending from the Plurality of Suffrages; much less, can they pretend to a legislative Power vested in them so as to impose what Laws or Canons they please upon the Church. But, they may be considered no otherwise than Men deputed by the Churches for the examining the true Grounds of the Controversies laid before them, and for searching for the Decision of them in the Holy Scripture; So that these Churches are not obliged to acquiesce in this Decision any further than they find it agreeable to the Word of God. For it may chance to fall out so that a Controversie which appears at first sight very intricate and difficult, afterwards being well weighed and the Reasons thereof duly examined on both sides, is very plain and easy to be determined. But if any moral Decrees are made by a Council, the same are to be taken to have no obliging Power, but what proceeds either from a preceding Commission and Authority, or from the Approbation of these Churches; so that Councils have no coercive Power over the Church. I cannot but touch, by the by, upon this Head, *viz.* that this Assertion; *The Council is above the Pope,* is of such a Nature as will easily gain credit with all that are guided by right Reason, or the Scriptures. For, who can be so stupid as not to be sensible, that a great many learned Men, who with joint labour apply themselves to the search after Truth, are to be preferred before the Judgment of one single Person, and that oftentimes of such a one, who has but a very indifferent insight into the Holy Scriptures and Divinity. This seems to imply somewhat of a Contradiction, that this Point is asserted by the self-same People, who make the Papal Chair the Center of the Church, and the Pope the Oecumenick Bishop: For, the *Romish*

Church pretends to be a Monarchical State; but this Assertion of the Superiority of the Councils, favours most of an Aristocracy. But this Riddle may be unfolded in a few Words: The *French* Clergy allows the Pope to be the Supream Head of the Church, as far as they find it suitable with their Interest. But whenever he attempts any thing against them, or the States Policy of that Kingdom, the old Song of the Liberty of the *Gallican* Church, and the antient Doctrine of the *Sorbone* is revived, which serves the *French* Clergy now and then for a Pretext, to persuade the vulgar sort of People, that the *Gallican* Church has not been polluted with those gross and abominable Errours as are introduced in the Church of *Rome*.[185] The next thing to be considered is, that it is most evident, that if a Controversie arises, which may be decided within the Body of one Church, there is no Occasion for the Communicating in such a Point with other Churches; And, that, in case one Church alone is not stock'd sufficiently with able Teachers for the composing of the Difference, and therefore must call to its Aid those of other Churches, it is superfluous to call together a greater number than may be sufficient for the accomplishment of the Work. So did the Church of *Antioch* refer the whole Controversie to those of *Jerusalem,* without giving the least Trouble to those of *Phoenice* and *Samaria,* though their Deputies passed in their Way thither through both these Places. Besides this, the Deputies that are sent, ought to receive their Authority and Instruction from their several Churches, whom they represent, because no Church has without reserve submitted herself to the Determination of her Teachers, but only as far as their Doctrine is agreeable to the Word of God. Neither are the Words in the Epistle to the *Hebr. c.* 13:17. to be understood any otherwise

---

185. The nationalistic ecclesiastical movement in France was called *Gallicanism.* Louis XIV claimed that the French monarch could limit papal authority. In 1682 an assembly of the French clergy met in Paris and adopted the Four Gallican Articles, which had been drafted by Jacques-Bénigne Bossuet. The articles asserted the king's independence from Rome in secular matters and proclaimed that, in matters of faith, the pope's judgment was not to be regarded as infallible without the assent of the whole church. [SZu]

than with this Limitation. Besides this, it is absolutely requisite that such Persons as have raised a Controversie should be heard in the Council, that their Reasons should be duely examined, weighed, and proceeded upon, according to the Rules prescribed in the Holy Writ. And if the Controversie does not barely concern a Point of Doctrine, but implies a Temporal Interest, those that have any Share in it cannot pretend to a Power of deciding the Point in Prejudice of the adverse Party. From whence it is evident, that the Points in question betwixt the Protestant Church and the Papal Chair cannot be composed by any Council, their Difference arising not barely from Point of Doctrine, but about Domination, Temporal Dignities, and vast Revenues. Nor is there the least Probability of any Composition betwixt these two Parties by way of Arbitration; For who is it that can pretend to decide so great a Point? Who is likely to be accepted of as an Arbitrator by both Parties? The Protestants, in all likelihood, will not be so foolish as to submit themselves and their Case to the Determination of any Assembly consisting all of *Roman* Catholicks their sworn Enemies; nor can they have the Imprudence as to ask it. And as for the Pope, he likes his Station too well, to put it to the Hazard of an Arbitration. But if an Assembly should be proposed to consist of an equal Number chosen by each Party, this Expedient would scarce take, it being to be feared that they would scarce keep within the bounds of Moderation, and that the Assembly would appear sometimes not unlike the Feast of the Centaures.

In what condition the Churches were under the Pagan Emperours.

§39. It having been hitherto demonstrated at large, that the Church is no State, we must consider in the next place, unto what kind of moral Bodies the Churches have the nearest relation, as they were in primitive Times under the Pagan Princes. It is evident enough, That they were of the nature of Colledges, or such Societies, where a great many are joined for the carrying on a certain Business, under this limitation nevertheless, as not to be independent from the Civil Jurisdiction. Concerning the nature of the Colledges and Corporations, *Jacobus Cujachus* may be consulted before all others, 7 *Observ.* 30, and 16; and

Observ. 3, and 5.[186] And it is here very well worth our most particular Observation, that such Societies as were erected for the exercise of Religion were by Publick Authority allowed of in the antient *Roman* Empire. This is attested among a great many others, by *Athanagoras,* in the beginning of his Apology for the Christians, when he says: *It is by your Command, you greatest of Princes, that several Nations live according to their own Customs and Laws, and every one, without being controuled by any Penal Statutes, freely exercise the same Religion in which he was educated.* And thus he proceeds immediately after: *All Mankind offer their Sacrifices, and use other Religious Ceremonies, according to the Custom of their Native Country.*[187] This Liberty of Conscience was, among others, the true cause, why the Christian Religion in so short a time did spread it self all over so vast an Empire, and why in the beginning, very few opposed its Progress, the Magistrates not thinking it belonging to their Province to intermeddle with it. And this is one Reason, why we never read of the Apostles having desired leave from the Civil Magistrates to preach the Gospel, or to plant a Church. Tho' another Reason may be given, why the Apostles were not obliged to ask leave from the Civil Magistrates for the Constituting of Christian Churches; because the Apostles had received their immediate Authority of Preaching the Gospel from him, who is the *King of kings,* and by whose Command all Mankind were then called to repentance.[188] From what has been said, this rational Conclusion may be drawn; That the Apostles had not only a Power to plant Churches in all places, where they found their Auditors inclined to receive the Doctrine of the Gospel, but that, also in all other places, whither this Doctrine was transplanted, the Believers might enter into such a Society, or plant a Church upon their own accord, without any Commission or Permis-

186. Jacobus Cujachus, i.e., Jacques Cujas, *Observationum Libri XVIII,* 1618, book 7, chap. 30: "De collegiis" (On Colleges). [SZu]

187. Athenagoras, *A Plea for the Christians* (*Presbeia peri Christianon; Apologia pro Christianis,* c. A.D. 177), chap. 1. See note 51, above. [SZu]

188. Acts 17:30. [Puf.]

sion for so doing, from the Apostles; but, that, pursuant to our Saviour's Expression, it was sufficient, if two or three were inclined to meet in his Name. If we trace the true nature of these Societies, which are constituted by a free Choice and Consent of certain Men, we may easily find to contain, all of them, something resembling a Democracy, where such Matters as concern the whole Body of the Society are to be dispatched by common Consent, and where no particular Person can claim any further Power over the rest, than what he has received by their joint Consent. From whence it may be rationally concluded, that at the first beginning, the Power of Constituting Teachers, and other Ministers of the Church, was originally lodged in the whole Church, or, the whole Congregation of the Believers. And, tho' it is unquestionable, that in the first primitive Church, Teachers were constituted by the Apostles in a great many places; nevertheless the *Greek* word χειροτονεῖν, (which implies something of a Democracy, and is often used in the Scriptures in this Case) argues sufficiently, that this was not done without the Approbation of the Church. It would be a hard Task to prove, that the Apostles did constitute Teachers themselves in all lesser Towns, or that they preached the Gospel in all lesser Places and Villages. It seems rather probable, that the Gospel was published by the Apostles in great Cities, and other places of note; from whence it was communicated unto other Places; and, that such Churches, as were not provided with Teachers, Bishops, or Presbyters by the Apostles themselves, or their special Authority, used either to chuse those very Persons to that Function, who were the first Preachers of the Gospel among them, or any others, whom they esteemed to be endowed, before others, with the Gift of Teaching. If we consult the Epistle of St. *Paul* to the *Romans,* it seems that the Gospel had been taught at *Rome,* before ever *Peter* and *Paul* came thither;[189] And the High Treasurer of the Queen *Candaces,* who is generally believed to have first carried the Doctrine of the Gospel to *Aethiopia,* and to have been the first Founder of the Christian Churches in those Parts, received no

189. Rom. 16.

Ordination as a Bishop or Presbyter from *Philip,* after his Baptism.[190] Neither did Christ or his Apostles prescribe any certain Form, to be used in the Ordination of Bishops, as he did in the use of the Sacraments; which seems to prove that for the obtaining of this Function, there is nothing more required, than for the Person to be called by the Church, and to have the Gift of Teaching. It is not to be denied, but that the Ordination of Ministers, and Imposition of Hands by the Bishops and Presbyters[191] is a very laudable and useful Ceremony, and ought to be received as such, with this restriction nevertheless, that the same need not to be deemed so absolutely necessary, as if without it no Person ought to be taken for a true Minister of the Church; especially since these miraculous Gifts which accompanied that Ceremony in the Infancy of the Primitive Church are many Ages past, become useless. The Church, like all other Colledges, have power to collect Stipends for their Ministers, and to make Collections for the Use of the Poor; but in a different degree from that which belongs to Civil Magistrates or Sovereigns, who levy Taxes, and have a Power to force their Subjects to a compliance with their Commands; But, in the Church this Power is founded upon the meer Liberality and free Consent of all the Believers in general, who being made sensible of their Duty of paying a Workman his Stipend, and relieving those in Distress, ought not to refuse such Acts of Justice and Humanity.[192] It properly belongs to all Colledges as well as Churches, to have a Power to make, with joint Consent of their Members, such Statutes, as may conduce towards the obtaining the Ends of their Society, provided they do not interfere with the legal Rights of their Sovereigns. Of this kind are these Statutes, which St. *Paul* recommends to the *Corinthians* in his first Epistle, in the 7 *Chaps.* If any one acted contrary to these Rules, he deservedly was to receive Correction, or to undergo such a Penalty as was dictated by the Statute, and which was to be laid upon him not by Vertue of an Inherent Power in the Colledge, but pursuant to their

190. Acts 8:27ff.
191. 1 Tim. 4:14.
192. 2 Cor. 8:2, 3; 9:5, 6, 7.

Contract. And, tho' Colledges have not any Power or Jurisdiction over their Members, unless what is absolutely requisite for the obtaining the true end of each Society, or else has been granted to them by their Sovereigns; Nevertheless, it is often practised in these Societies, and may be done without prejudice to the Rights of their Sovereigns, that, if any Differences arise betwixt the Members of one and the same Colledge, these are composed by the Interposition and Arbitration of the rest of the Members of that Colledge or Society, to the End, that a mutual good Correspondency may be cultivated among them. In which sense is to be taken the Admonition which St. *Paul* gives to the *Corinthians* concerning this point in the 1 Epistle, in the 6 *Chapter*, in the first and following *Verses*. Lastly, because many Vices were at the time of the first publishing of the Gospel in vogue among the Heathens, which were not punishable by the Pagan Laws, they being more encouraged to the observance of Moral Duty by the prospect of Honours than by any civil Commands; And, the Christians believing it more peculiarly belonging to themselves to recommend and adorn their Profession by a holy Life, and, by an innocent Conversation, to excel the Heathens, some Statutes were, at the very beginning, introduced into the Primitive Church, which were thought most convenient to correct all manner of Licentiousness, according to St. *Paul's* Direction: *If any one that is called a Brother be a Fornicator, or Covetous, or an Idolater, or a Railer, or a Drunkard, or an Extortioner, with such a one do not eat.*[193] From whence it appears, that in the primitive Times, Church Censure was used in the Churches, all which may easily be supposed to have been done without the least prejudice to the Sovereign Power, it being always for the Interest of the State, that Subjects should lead an innocent Life. It is worth our Observation, that the Punishments inflicted by vertue of these Statutes, were of such a nature, as might be put in execution without the least prejudice to the Civil Government; such were private Admonitions, publick Reprimands, and Church Penances, the extream Remedy was Excommunication, by

193. 1 Cor. 6:9, 10; 1 Tim. 5:20. [Puf.]

vertue of which, a Member of the Church was either for a time deprived from enjoying the benefit of the Publick Worship, or entirely excluded from being a Member of the Church. This being the utmost, unto which any Colledge can pretend, *viz.* entirely to exclude a Member of their Society. This Exclusion, tho' in it self considered, of the greatest moment, (since thereby a Christian was deprived of the whole Communion with the Church) Nevertheles did not alter the Civil State or Condition of a Subject; But those that were thus excommunicated suffered no loss in their Dignities, Honour, Rights, or Fortunes. For, that the Church Censures should extend to the real Prejudice of the civil Condition of any Subject, is not any ways requisite for the obtaining the Ends for which the Church is Established; Neither can it be supposed, that without defrauding Sovereigns of their Right, such a Power can be exercised over Subjects, unless with their own Consent, and by vertue of a publick Civil Authority.

§40. The next thing which deserves our Consideration is, whether the Church is, and how far it received any Alteration from its former Condition, after Princes, whole Kingdoms, and States did profess the Christian Religion. Where it is to be observed, That the Churches did thereby not receive any essential Perfection; it being evident, that the Christian Religion could be exercised, and subsist without the State; and Commonwealths did not depend from the Christian Religion; The scope of the Christian Religion, and of civil Governments, being quite different in their own nature. For, *our* πολιτευμα, *our Conversation is in Heaven; and, if in this Life only we have hope in Christ, we are of all Men most miserable.*[194] For this Reason it was, that the Apostles were never forward to appear before Princes, tho' they might have obtained an easie Access by their miraculous Deeds. So *Herod* was exceeding glad when he saw *Jesus,* because he hoped to have seen some Miracle done by him.[195] But they were very cautious in this point, lest it might appear to some, as if the Gospel wanted to be maintained by Human

Concerning the condition of the Church under Christian Princes.

194. Philipp. 3:20; 2 Cor. 5:2, 8; 1 Cor. 15:19.
195. Luke 23:8.

Strength, or that perhaps those Princes might pretend to a greater Authority over them, than was consistent with the safety of the Christian Religion. Notwithstanding all this, the Christian Religion does not in any wise impair or ecclipse the legal Rights of Sovereigns, but rather confirms and establishes the civil Power, as is apparent out of several passages in the holy Scripture.[196] If it should be granted that the Church was a State independent from any temporal Jurisdiction, the consequence would be this, That the civil Power could not but receive a most remarkable Limitation and Diminution, and the condition of a Subject must receive a great alteration; whereas on the other hand, the condition of Christians, or of Teachers in the Church (considered as such) is neither abolished nor altered, because either the Prince, or the Subjects in general do receive the Christian Faith, there being not the least footstep to be met withal in the Scriptures, implying any such alteration: Besides this, there is not any express Command in the New Testament, directed to Sovereigns, which entitles them to any particular Prerogative in the Church, like to that which the Kings of *Israel* had received in the 17 *Chap.* of *Deuteronomy:* From whence arises this conclusion, that, what right Sovereigns can claim in the Church, and Church Affairs, must be deduced, either out of the natural constitution of the civil Power, or out of the true Genius of the Christian Religion, or else must owe its off-spring to the free consent of the Church.

Churches do not alter their nature of being a Colledge. §41. Out of what has been laid down, it appears first of all, that, if a Prince or whole Commonwealth, do receive the Doctrine of Christ, the Church does thereby not receive any other Alteration, as to her natural Constitution, but that, whereas she was formerly to be considered only as a private Society or Colledge, yet such a one as being subordinate to the Law, and therefore to be cherished by the Higher Powers, who had no legal Right to disturb, prosecute or destroy it; She now being put under the particular Protection of her Sovereigns, enjoys a greater share of Security, and is beyond the reach of the Persecutions

---

196. Matt. 22:21; John 9:11; Rom. 13:1ff.; 1 Cor. 15:24; 1 Tim. 2:1, 2; 1 Pet. 2:13, 14.

of the Infidels. Notwithstanding this, the Church is thereby not exalted from a Colledge to a State, since, by the receiving of the Christian Religion, the civil Government does not undergo any Alteration or Diminution; On the contrary, Sovereigns loose nothing of their legal Rights, neither are Subjects in any wise absolved from their Duties and Obligations. For it implies a contradiction, that a double Sovereignty, and two different sorts of Obligations in the Subject should be lodged in one and the same Commonwealth. It is a frivolous Objection, that the Church and civil Government have different Ends and Objects, not repugnant to one another; For, from thence is not to be inferred, that the Church must be a State, or that the Christian Religion cannot be propagated, maintained or exercised, without the Church assume the same Power that belongs to the civil Government. In these places therefore, where the whole People and the Prince profess the Christian Religion, the Commonwealth receives the Church into its Protection, and, tho' strictly united, there is no collision or emulation betwixt them, nor does either of them receive any prejudice in their respective Rights, but without the least Interference with one another, the Church remains a Colledge, whereof the Prince, and all the Subjects are now become Members. So, that each Subject, besides the Person he represented in the State, has assumed that of a Christian, and in this respect is esteemed a Member of the Church. Neither is every one to be considered in the Church according to the Station or Dignity he bears in the Commonwealth, but, these Qualifications are, as it were, laid aside there, and he is only regarded as a Christian. So, that the General of an Army cannot claim any Prerogative to himself in the Church beyond the private Centinel. And it is past all doubt, that one and the same Man may represent several Persons, according to the several Functions and Obligations belonging to him.

§42. It is also, according to my Opinion, beyond question, that Kings, Princes, or other civil Magistrates, by receiving the Christian Doctrine, are not constituted Bishops or Teachers in the Church, this Function not properly belonging to every Christian, but only to such as have a lawful Vocation, and are fitly qualified for it. Besides this, the Royal Office and that of Teachers are of such a nature, that they cannot

Princes are thereby not made Bishops.

conveniently be Administred by one and the same Person, not, because of any natural repugnancy betwixt them, but that each of them is involved in such a multitude of Trouble and variety of Business, that it cannot rationally be supposed for one Man to be able to undergo such a Fatigue. It is no less evident, that Sovereigns, by becoming Christians, are not authorised to alter the Ministry of the Church, or to order it at pleasure, or to force the Ministers of the Gospel to teach any Doctrine which is not founded in the Scriptures, or to preach up Human Inventions for Articles of Faith. For, what, and how Ministers ought to Teach, is prescribed by God himself, who expects an exact Obedience in this Point, as well from Kings as other Christians. And it is to be considered, that whenever Princes receive the Christian Doctrine, the Teachers, notwithstanding this, remain in their former Station as to their Duty and Obligation to God, as well, as all the rest of their Christian Subjects, who having received their Instructions, as to their Religion, only from God, without the assistance of their Sovereigns, these cannot claim any right to impose any thing of this kind upon them.

Concerning the Duty and Right of Christian Princes of defending the Church.

§43. Notwithstanding all this, it is not to be supposed that Sovereigns, by becoming Christians, have acquir'd no peculiar Rights, or have not a more particular Duty laid upon them than before; There being certain Obligations, which owe their off-spring to the union of that Duty, which is incumbent to every Christian, with that of the Royal Office. The first and chiefest of these Obligations seems to be, that Sovereigns ought to be Defenders of the Church, which they are oblig'd to protect not only against all such of their Subjects, as dare to attempt any thing against it, but also against Foreigners, who pretend to be injurious to their Subjects upon that score. And, tho' the Christian Doctrine is not to be propagated by violence or force of Arms, and our Saviour has highly recommended Patience and Sufferings as peculiar Vertues belonging to Christians, Princes are nevertheless not debarr'd from their Right of Protecting the Christian Religion by all lawful means, and Patience ought not to take place here, except when no other lawful means can secure us against our Enemies. So we see that St. *Paul* saved himself from being scourged by declaring himself to be a *Roman,* and escaped the Fury of the *Jews* by making his Appeal to the Emperour.[197] And our Saviour himself left this Advice to his Disciples, That *when they were persecuted in one City, they should fly into another.*[198] And, it being an incumbent Duty belonging to all Sovereigns, to defend their Subjects against all violence; they ought to take more effectual care that they do not suffer any Injuries for the Christian Religions sake; for, what could be more reproachful to a Christian Prince, than that his Subjects should be sufferers upon that account? The next care which belongs to Christian Princes, is, to provide necessary Revenues for the exercise of the Christian Religion. For as has been shewn before, that no other Patrimony belonged to the Primitive Church, but the Alms and free Contributions of the Believers, and that these cannot but be supposed to be very uncertain, the Ministers and Teachers in the Church run no small hazard of being exposed to want, if they have nothing else to rely upon, but the bare contributions of the Congregation, who being in some places poor, and Subject to other Taxes, are incapable of supplying their want. And, not to dissemble the Truth, after Princes and entire States have received the Doctrine of Christ, it would appear very ill, that, whereas they enjoy such ample Revenues, they would deal so sparingly with the Church, the more, because it is a general Maxim among Men, to value a Function according to its Revenues. What St. *Paul* recommends to the *Romans* in the 15th *Chapter, v.* 27. and in the 1 Epist. to the *Corinthians* 9:11. ought to be the more taken notice of by Christian Princes, because they can with less difficulty, or any sensible injury to themselves, put it in practise in their Station, they having the management of the Publick Revenues in their hands. It cannot be denied, but that too vast Revenues are not always useful to Ministers of the Church, and prove sometimes prejudicial both to Church and State; and that such as make profession of the Ministry of the Gospel, ought not to make a Trade of their Function, or to think it their main Business to gather Riches, and take the Min-

197. Acts 22:25.
198. Matt. 10:23.

istry for their By-work; nevertheless, if it be duely considered, that he who cordially (as he ought to do) applies himself to the Ministerial Function, has no other ways left him to provide for his Family; and that the vulgar Sort scarce pay a due Respect to a Minister, unless they see him live handsomely and well; whereas he, who is starv'd by his Function is the May-Game of the common People, unto whom may be applied that old Saying of the Poet; *That this Man appears to be the Servant of a poor and wretched Lord. Apparet servum hunc esse Domini pauperis miserique.* Princes ought therefore to look upon this as one main part of their Devotion, to settle certain and constant Sallaries or Revenues upon the Ministers of the Church, as much as may be, at least sufficient for their Maintainance. In the Old Testament the Priests were to live from the Altar, but those of the best kind were brought to the Altar.[199] Besides this, Princes ought not only to take care of Church-Buildings, but also to erect and maintain Schools, which being the Seminaries both of the Church and State, if the first Rudiments of Christianity be not implanted in the Schools, it cannot scarce be expected, that Men, when grown up, should receive much benefit by publick Sermons.

Concerning the rights of Princes, as to Ecclesiastical Affairs. And first, of the general Inspection.

§44. But among other Considerations, as to what Rights properly belong to Princes as to Ecclesiastical Affairs, it is evident, that, since by the Doctrine of the Gospel the Civil Power is in no wise impaired, and a Prince cherishes a Church under his Jurisdiction, he legally claims a Right of having a general Inspection over this as well as all other Societies; at least, so far as to take care that nothing be transacted in these Colledges to his Prejudice. For Mankind being so perverse in its Nature, that in Matters, even the most Sacred, if managed without controul, they seldom let it slip through their hands without a Stain; And that therefore it is scarce to be questioned, but the Christian Doctrine is subject to the same Corruption, and that under Pretence of Religion many pernicious Designs may be hatched against the Interest of the Commonwealth. A Prince in whose Territories a Church is planted, if

199. Galat. 6:6; 2 Tim. 2:6.

he afterwards enters into the Communion of that Church, has questionless a Right to examin what Matters, and in what Manner they are transacted in the Convention of their Presbyters, or in their Ecclesiastical Courts, if there be any such among them; Whether they do not transgress their Bounds? whether they act according to the Civil Laws, or whether they do not assume to themselves a Power to determine such Cases as properly belong to the Civil Jurisdiction? Of this Kind are Matrimonial Cases, which without Reason, and upon very slender Pretences, the Priests have drawn under their Jurisdiction, to the great Prejudice of the Sovereign Power; For, it being an unquestionable Right belonging to Sovereigns to constitute Laws concerning Matrimonial Cases, according to the Law of Nature and of God, I cannot see any Reason why they have not a Right to determine Matrimonial Differences. And because the Ministers of the Church make use of Church-discipline, the Prince may make a legal Enquiry whether, under Pretence of these Rules prescribed by our Saviour, they do not introduce Novelties, which may prove prejudicial to the State? And as these Enchroachments are no essential Part of the Christian Doctrine, but rather to be looked upon like Spots which disguise its natural Beauty; So, I cannot see with what Face it can be denied, that those ought to be taken off, especially by the Authority of those whose Interest is most nearly concerned; unless they have Impudence enough to own, that the Christian Religion may lawfully be misapplied to By-uses. And let it be granted, that every thing is transacted as it ought to be in these Conventions of the Presbyters, Consistories or Episcopal Courts, why should they be asham'd or angry at their Sovereigns taking Cognisance of their Proceedings. And this Right of Inspection does never cease after the Sovereign has once entred into the Communion of the Church, it being his Duty to take care that no Abuses may creep into the Church, in process of Time, that may endanger the State.

§45. Because the Right of Constituting Ministers of the Church does originally belong to the whole Congregation the Prince must needs have his Share in it, as being a Member of the Congregation; I say his Share: For it is not reasonable that a Minister should be forced upon any Church against their Consent, and without their Approbation,

Concerning the Right of Princes, as to Church Ministers.

except it be for very weighty Reasons. For, the Right of Constituting Ministers in the Church does not belong to the Prince in the same manner, as it is his Prerogative to constitute Civil Magistrates and other Publick Ministers of State, which being a part of the Sovereign Power, cannot be called in question. But Teachers in the Church, considered meerly as such, are none of the King's Ministers, but Servants of Christ, and Ministers of the Church, not Officers of the State. And because, in the Primitive Church, Ministers used to be constituted by χειροτονίαν, or by the Suffrages of the Christians, the Prince may lawfully claim his Vote in the same Church whereof he is a Member; But as for the other Churches under his Jurisdiction, they ought to be left to their free Choice, exept there be some prevailing Reasons, which oblige the Prince to interpose his Authority; it being unjust, that a Minister should be put upon a Church against their Will, if they can alledge any lawful Exception against him. For, a Teacher thus forced upon his Auditors, for whom they have neither esteem nor Love, is likely to edifie but little by his Doctrine. Nevertheless, Sovereigns ought to have a watchful Eye over the Churches, and to take care that Persons not fitly qualified for this sacred Function, may not be promoted to the Ministry either by Simony or other unlawful Means: For though it is the Interest of the whole Church to provide against these Corruptions, Sovereigns are likely to do it with much better Success than can be expected from private Persons. They may authorise certain Persons to be present at these Elections, and who, by their Authority, may prevent all manner of Disorder or Corruption, and at the same time make a due enquiry, whether such Persons as are to be put into the Ministry are of an approved Life and Doctrine.[200] And, because the Ministers of the Church do sometimes act negligently or preposterously in their Office, which often proves the Occasion of Scandal and Schism in the Church,[201] Sovereigns may constitute over them Inspectors, with an Authority to reprove, and sometimes to punish such as transgress their Rules. But these Inspectors, being no less subject to human Frail-

---

200. 1 Tim. 3:10.
201. Rom. 16:17.

ties than other men, Care ought to be taken that their Authority be so limited as to be accountable of all their Proceedings, either to the Prince, or before a Consistory authorised for that purpose, if they transgress their Bounds or trespass upon the Ministers of the Church. As all these matters do contribute to the maintaining of good Order in the Church, and may best be put in execution by the Sovereign Authority; So it is manifest, that Princes, as they are chief Members of the Church, may justly claim this Prerogative as properly belonging to their high Station and Princely Office.

§46. In case of any Difference or Controversie concerning any Point of Doctrine which may sometimes arise in the Church, so that the Teachers are divided in their Opinions, it belongs to the Sovereign Authority to take care that these Differences may be composed, not only as the Sovereign is a Member of the Church, but as he is the Supream Head of the Commonwealth; It having been frequently observed, that Differences of Opinions and Animosities of the Parties concerned, cause great Commotions in the State. Upon such Occasions Sovereigns have a Right to call together an Assembly of the most able Divines, and to authorise them to examine the Controversie, and to determine it according to the Tenure of the Scriptures; The Supream Direction of this Assembly ought to be managed by the Prince's Authority; For, since it can scarce be supposed that matters should be transacted there without Heats and Animosities, it will be both for the Honour and Interest of this Assembly, if by the Presence of certain Persons well versed in Business, these Heats be allayed, and matters carried on with an equal Temperament. Neither do I see how any one besides the Prince can lay claim to this Power of calling such an Assembly; for, put the case, that one Party should refuse to appear, and to submit unto the other's Direction, which way will they be able to compel them to it? And who is it, that can with less Difficulty put in execution the Decrees of such a Synod, than he, who has the Sovereign Power in his Hands? Tho' at the same time it ought not to be forgotten, that this Power must not extend it self beyond its due Bounds, but be suitable to the Genius of the Christian Religion. But, in case Divines

Concerning the Right of calling together a Synod.

out of other Countries are to be called unto this Convocation or Assembly, it is, I think, a plain case, that these cannot appear there without leave first obtained from their Sovereigns. And if a Council should be called, consisting of selected Divines out of a great many Commonwealths, this cannot be done without a foregoing Agreement made betwixt those Sovereigns that are concerned therein. For it is not allowable for Subjects of another State to come to us upon such an Account, nor can ours go to them upon such an Errand, unless by joint Consent of the higher Powers. And since Sovereigns cannot claim any Jurisdiction over one another, there will be no place left for any Prerogative, but Matters must be transacted according to mutual Contract.

§47. For what Reasons the Primitive Christians did introduce Church Discipline, *viz.* to be distinguished from the Heathens by their holy Life and Conversation, and to supply the Defects of the civil Pagan Laws, which did not restrain them from such Vices as were abominable to the Christians, has been sufficiently explained before. This Reason takes no more place now, after whole Commonwealths as well as their Sovereigns are entred into the Communion of the Christian Church; for there is not the same Occasion now to be distinguished from the Heathens by an unspotted Conversation, after the rooting out of the Pagan Religion, all Christians being under an equal Obligation to endeavour an unblemished Life. But, notwithstanding the general Conversion of whole Commonwealths to the Christian Faith, care ought to be taken, that Holiness of Life be not laid aside among Christians; from whence arises this Question: Whether it be better to make use of the antient Church Discipline now, in the same manner as it was practised in the Primitive times? Or, whether it be not more expedient to admit of some Alterations, after Sovereigns are entred into the Communion of the Church? The last of these two seems to be most probable; because this antient Church Discipline which was introduced for a certain time, to supply the deficiency of the Pagan Laws, and to amend their vicious Lives and Conversation, and was thus left to the direction of certain People, is not an Essential part of Christianity; and,

Their Right concerning Church-Discipline.

besides this, carries this Inconveniency along with it, that it may easily degenerate into a kind of a pretended Soveraignty, and prove prejudicial to the Civil Power. And, as Soveraigns have a Right to provide against every thing that may be the probable cause of Convulsions in the State; so may this defect be supplied by the Civil Laws, and Vices may be suppressed by Civil Punishments. Neither do I see any reason to the contrary, why Vices should not be as easily corrected by Punishments prescribed by the Civil Laws, as by Church-Censures; or, why the first should not prove as effectual as the latter for the suppressing of Publick Scandals? It will perhaps be objected, That Ecclesiastical Discipline has a much greater Influence over Christians towards the amendment of their Lives, than Civil Punishments; because the first penetrates into the Heart; whereas Civil Punishments do not touch us but superficially: Unto this it may be answered, That Church-Discipline does not always answer this end, it being not to be doubted, but that some Men, tho' they undergo all the Church-Penances, retain in their hearts the same vicious Inclinations, or sometimes grow more stubborn and bold. But if it be taken as an Expiation for our Sins in regard of God Almighty, it is to be observed, that if we pretend to an Expiation for any Trespasses, which fall under the cognizance of Humane Laws, we must therein be directed by the Word of God, which does not prescribe Church-Penance as a proper Satisfaction in this case. For our sins are not remitted, because we have undergone Church-Penance, but because our Hearts are purified by the Blood of Christ, provided we, by the Faith, apply his Sufferings unto us. But, supposing it should be thought most convenient, that some sort of Vices ought to be corrected by Church-Discipline, the best Expedient would be, to leave it first to the determination of the Civil Judges, who, according to the Circumstances of the Case, ought to send the Delinquents to the Ecclesiastical Court, there to undergo the Church-Censure. For, Christian Soveraigns have an unquestionable Right to determine, what sort of Misdemeanors are punishable by the Civil Laws, and which of them come under the Cognizance of Ecclesiastical Courts; and consequently, to decree, what sort of Church-Censure ought to be laid upon the Delinquents, according to the different Nature of the Trespass; which may be put in Execution by the Ministers accordingly. Concerning Excommunication, the same ought not to be put in Practice, but, with this caution, that it ought not to be left to the discretion of Priests, so as to be inflicted by them at pleasure; but this Power ought to be limited by certain Rules prescribed by those that have the Legislative Power in a State. For, in a Christian Commonwealth Excommunication alters the Civil Condition of a Subject, and renders him infamous and detestable among his fellow-Christians: And as it affects the Civil State of Subjects, Soveraigns, unless they will let others encroach upon their Prerogative, ought to determine concerning its Legality.

Concerning the Power of making Ecclesiastical Canons or Statutes.

§48. Since the Christian Religion does not in any wise diminish the Rights of Soveraigns, these, if entred into the Communion of the Church, have a Power to examine, what Canons or Ecclesiastical Statutes are received in the Church; and if some of them are found superfluous, or interfering with the Sovereign Power, to abolish the same; and if there appears any deficiency, to supply what is wanting towards the maintaining a good Order, and the Glory of the Church (which however, ought not to be done without the Advice, at least, of the chief Men of the Church) and lastly, give to those Statutes the force of Civil Laws. This Power nevertheless, of making Ecclesiastical Statutes, must be exercised with a great deal of caution, the same being limited to the outward form of the Church-Government, and to maintain its Order and Decency, Christians being not to be over-heap'd with a vast number of Canons.[202] For, those that stretch the Power of Soveraigns to such a pitch, as to make them the absolute Judges of the Christian Religion, and to attribute to them a Right of establishing certain Articles of Faith by Civil Laws, or to annex to them a force equal to the Civil Constitutions, and to force upon their Subjects a certain Religion, under severe Penalties, or oblige them either to profess or to deny certain Points of Doctrine, which are controverted amongst Christians; These, I say, act quite contrary to the true Genius of the Christian

---

202. Coloss. 2:16, 21, 22, 23; 1 Tim. 4:34.

Religion, and to the Method made use of by Christ and his Apostles, for the propagating of this Doctrine; They destroy the very Essential part of our Faith, which being a Gift of the Holy Ghost, and a Belief founded in our Hearts, is transmuted into an outward Confession, where the Tongue, to avoid Temporal Punishment, is forced to speak those things which are in no wise agreeable to the Heart. This however admits again of a Limitation; For herein are not comprehended these Points, which proceeding from Natural Religion, are also contained in the Christian Doctrine, and all of them imply a profound Reverence to be paid to the Supream BEING. For, it is beyond all question, that those that act against the very Dictates of Reason, ought to be subject to Civil Punishments, since they strike at the very Foundation of Civil Societies: Such are Idolatry, Blasphemy, Profanation of the Sabbath; where nevertheless great care is to be taken, that a due difference be made betwixt the Moral part of that Precept concerning the Sabbath, which is unalterable, and the Ceremonial part of it. Princes therefore at their first entrance into the Communion of the Christian Church, might Lawfully destroy the Images and Temples of the Idols, and the Groves, and other Meeting places dedicated to their superstitious Worship. Neither can it be called in question, but that Christian Soveraigns have a Right to inflict Civil Punishments upon such as revile the whole System of the Christian Religion, and ridicule the Mysteries of the Christian Faith, at least, they may Banish them the Country. But for the rest, it is in vain to believe, that the true enlightning of our Mind, and the inward consent to such Articles of Faith as surpass our Understanding, can be procured by violent means, or temporal punishments. For, supposing you force a Man to dissemble his thoughts, to speak contrary to what he conceives in his own Opinion, let his Confession be never so formal, and his Gestures never so well composed and conformable to certain prescribed Rules, this has not the least affinity with true Religion, unless he at the same time does feel an inward motion, and hearty compliance with what he professes. Neither ought People, according to the true Genius of the Doctrine of Christ, be enticed to receive the Christian Religion by Temporal Interest, Honours, or other such like Advantages; for, Christ did promise, that those that followed him, should receive their Reward in the life to come, but fore-told them nothing but Crosses and Tribulations in this. And, those that embrace any Religion out of a Motive of Temporal Advantages, do plainly shew, that they have a greater Value for their own interest than Religion. And certainly, scarce any body, that has but common sense, can perswade himself, that such a sort of Worship can be pleasing to God Almighty. Sovereigns being not constituted for Religion's sake, they cannot under that colour exact from their Subjects a blind Obedience in matters of Religion, it being unquestionable, that if Subjects should blindfold follow the Religion of their Sovereign, they cannot by all his Authority be assured of their Salvation; from whence it is evident, that, in case any Subject be fully convinced, that he can out of the Holy Scripture discover any Errors, which are crept into the Church, even that by Law established (especially concerning any Principal Point of Faith), he neither can, nor ought to be hindered in his design by the Sovereign Authority, before his Reasons be heard, and well debated in the presence of the best and ablest Judges; and, if by them he be legally and plainly convicted of his Error, then, and not before, ought he to be silenced. To force People into the Church by the bare Civil Authority, must needs fill the Commonwealth with Hypocrites, who cannot be supposed to Act according to the Dictates of their Consciences. For, since in Religious Matters an absolute Uniformity betwixt the Heart and Tongue is required, how can it otherwise be, but that such as profess a Religion disagreeable to their Opinion, should never be satisfied in their Consciences; when they consider, that they impose upon God Almighty.

What Prerogatives belong to Sovereigns, as being Protectors of the Publick Tranquility.

§49. The Care of preserving the Publick Peace, belonging in a most peculiar manner to Sovereigns, has furnished some with a specious Pretence to affirm, that since differences in Religion cause frequent Convulsions in the State, and it is to be deemed one of the greatest Happinesses of a Government, if its Subjects, in general, are of one Religion, all means, tho' never so violent, may be put in execution to extirpate these Differences in Religion. They alledge, that as much more precious our Souls are before our Bodies, the more Sovereigns are obliged to be watchful over them; and, that the true Love which a Sovereign bears to his Subjects, can never be more conspicuous, than when he takes effectual care of their Salvation. These, it must be confess'd, are very specious Pretences, and have sometimes had such powerful influence over Princes, who were else naturally not inclined to Severity, that they have nevertheless by these plausible Arguments been prevailed upon to assist with their Authority the cruel Designs of Priests. It will therefore not be beyond our scope, to make a strict Enquiry what account ought to be made of these so specious Reasons in a well constituted Government. In the first place then, it is to be considered, that it has been foretold by our Saviour, that there should always be in the Church Weeds amongst the Wheat; that is to say, that there should be false Doctrines raised in the Church; and these, according to the Commands of our Saviour, were not to be extirpated Root and Branch, but to be reserved for the Day of Judgment. For a Sovereign that takes to such violent courses, may make a havock among his Subjects, which commonly proves equally pernicious to the Innocent and Guilty; nevertheless, he will find it impracticable quite to abolish all Errors and Differences in the Church. Never did any body shew a greater Love to Mankind than our Saviour, who sacrificed himself for our Salvation; Yet he made use of no other ways to propagate his Doctrine, than Teaching, when he might have commanded Twelve Legions of Angels to force Mankind to Obedience. How can a Prince be esteemed to follow the Foot-steps of Christ, who makes such profligate Wretches as the Dragoons his Apostles, for the Conversion of his Subjects? That Pretence of the Love of Sovereigns toward their Subjects, let it be never so specious, he ought not under that colour endeavour to subvert or alter the Method of propagating the Christian Doctrine, according to the true Genius of the Christian Religion. Besides this, it is not absolutely necessary to maintain the Publick Tranquility, that all the Subjects in general should be of one Religion, or, which is the same in effect, the differences about some Points in Religion, considered barely as such, are not the true causes of Disturbances in a State; but the Heats and Animosities, Ambition and perverted Zeal of some, who make these Differences their Tools, wherewith they often raise Disturbances in the State. Such turbulent Spirits ought to be curbed, and care to be taken so to tye up their Hands, as that they want Power to influence the Minds of such Subjects, as otherwise would be well satisfied, to enjoy peaceably a Liberty of Conscience. And what should move a Prince to disturb his good Subjects meerly upon the score of Differences in Opinion, as long as they live quietly under his Government? For, supposing their Opinion to be erroneous, it is not at his, but their own Peril, and they alone must be answerable for it. For, in my Opinion, Sovereigns are entrusted with the Sword, wherewith to dissect Controversies, as *Alexander* did with the *Gordian* Knot. But, that it may not be objected as if I intended to encourage all sorts of Heresies and Licentiousness, I do declare, that this is far different from my purpose, but that on the contrary, it is to be wished, and ought to be endeavoured, to procure but one Faith and Religion in a State, and especially such a one as is absolutely agreeable to the Doctrine of Christ and his Apostles, contained in the Holy Scripture; such a one as cannot but contribute towards the maintaining of the Publick Tranquility. For, I do not think, that all Uniformity in Religion is equally capable of procuring that Union; neither can the Pagan Religion, *Mahometans, Arians, Anabaptists,* and that of *Antichrist* himself, claim that Prerogative, but only the true and antient Religion contained in the Holy Scripture. For, this is only to be deemed the truly Antient Religion, which is derived from the pure and genuine Spring of the Primitive Christian Religion. As among the *Jews,* such only could boast to follow the true foot-steps of Antiquity, as proved their Doctrine out of the Books of *Moses.* All what degenerates from the Nature of its genuine Spring, tho' back'd by the Traditions of some Ages, being only to be look'd upon as an inveterate Error. Princes being then Protectors of the Publick Tranquility, have an Authority to inspect what Canons are received into the Church, and to cause them to be examined according to the true Tenure of the Holy Scripture; and this care is not to be committed to the management of a few, who may perhaps be swayed by Faction or Interest, but to all such as have a solid knowledge of the Holy Scripture. If every thing be found consonant to its Rules, then may a Sovereign by his Authority Command this Doctrine to be

Taught both in publick and private. But where there is not any Publick Form of Religion established in a Commonwealth, it is the Sovereign's care, that one may be composed by the assistance of such as are well versed in the Holy Scripture, which being approved of by the general consent of his Subjects, ought to be professed by all, and all those especially, who pretend to the Ministry, are to be tyed up to its Rules. This form of Worship being once received, a Prince may justly deny his Protection to all such as will not comply with it, unless he find it to be against the Common Interest of the Commonweal. If any one should undertake to contradict this Publick Form, especially in such Points as are the Heads of the Christian Religion, he ought to be admonished to desist, his Reasons, if he has any, to be examined, and when convicted of his Error, to be silenced; if all this prove fruitless, he may lawfully be banished. For, since, according to the Doctrine of the Apostles, we are to avoid the Conversation of Hereticks, it would be unreasonable that a whole Society of Men should fly from one or a few capricious Persons; So that he or they ought to seek out for a new Habitation, after they have been legally convicted of their Error; for fear they should spread their erroneous Doctrines further than may be consistent with the Publick Safety. But we allow no other Punishment in such a case, except their Doctrine should amount to Blasphemy.

§50. Notwithstanding what has been alledg'd there may be such a juncture of Time & Circumstances, that Sovereigns may, nay ought with a safe Conscience to tolerate such of their Subjects as are of a different Opinion from the Established Religion. For, it may so happen, that the number of the Dissenters is so great, as not to be expelled without great Prejudice to the State, and, not without danger to the Commonwealth, if they should settle under another Government. For that common Saying of a certain Sort of Men that 'tis better to have a Country lie waste, than to have it inhabited by Hereticks, favours of Barbarity, if not Inhumanity. And a certain Prince who said, that he would rather walk out of his Territories with nothing but a Staff in his hands, than to suffer it to be inhabited by Hereticks, may well pass for

Concerning Tolerating of several Religions in a State.

one of the most bigotted Zealots in Christendom. For the Doctrine of the Gospel is not destructive to civil Society, neither is thereby the least Obligation laid upon Princes, to propagate Religion by violent and destructive means, or to undertake more in that behalf, than belongs to them as Protectors of the publick Tranquility; they may therefore with a safe Conscience supercede such violent ways, by which the State either is endangered or weakned; especially, since neither our Saviour did make use of them himself, nor commanded any thing like it to his Apostles. On the other hand, those that expect to be tolerated in a State, ought by all means to endeavour to live peaceably and quietly, and as becomes good Subjects, they ought not to Teach any Doctrine which savours of Sedition and Disobedience, or to suffer such Principles to be fomented in their Congregations, as may prove destructive to the Prerogatives of their Sovereigns. For, there is not the least question to be made, but Princes have a right to rout out such as propagate these Doctrines, they having not the least relation to Religion, but are like spots, wherewith some turbulent Heads bespatter the Christian Religion. Besides this, there is another duty incumbent to Sovereigns over a State, where more than one Religion is tolerated; *viz.* to keep a watchful eye over them, that the Dissenting Parties do not break out into extravagant Expressions about the Differences in Religion, these being the Fuel that enflames them into Animosities, which oftentimes prove the spring of Factions, Troubles, and intestine Commotions. A much greater Obligation lies upon Sovereigns to tolerate Dissenters, if they, when they first submitted to the Government, had their Liberty of Conscience granted them by Contract; or have obtain'd it afterwards by certain Capitulations, any following Statutes, or by the fundamental Laws of the Land; all which ought to be sacred to Princes, and to be observed by them with the same Circumspection, as they expect a due Obedience from their Subjects. No Opinion concerning matter of Religion ought to be declared Erroneous, before it be duely examined, and the Parties convicted, especially if they are ready to prove the same out of the Fundamental Articles of the Christian Faith; And great care is to be taken that such a Decision be not left to the Management of their Adversaries, who being perhaps guided by self Interest, oftentimes are both Accusers and Judges. There are not a few Politicians, who are of opinion, that Sovereigns may with a safe Conscience give Protection to their Subjects, tho' of an erroneous Opinion, provided it be for the benefit of the Commonwealth, especially if care be taken, that they do not draw away others into the same Error. For, supposing the established Religion both in point of Doctrine and Morality, to excel all others, it is to be hoped that the Dissenting Parties may be in time brought over to it, rather than to be feared, that they should seduce others; Besides, that it may contribute to the encrease of the Zeal and Learning of the established Clergy, it being sufficiently proved by Experience, that in those places and times, where and when no Religious Differences were in agitation, the Clergy soon degenerated into Idleness and Barbarity.

§51. Furthermore, as Sovereigns in all other Matters of Moment ought to act with great Circumspection; so, especially in matters of Religion, they cannot proceed with too much caution, an injustice of this nature, being the most sensible of all that can be done to a Subject. For what can be more abominable, than to let Subjects suffer unjustly for their Faith in Christ, and that perhaps for no other reason, but, because some others out of self Interest, cannot agree with them in Opinion. And, if a Prince, who prompted by his own cruel Inclinations tyrannises over his Subjects, is odious to all the World, how much more abominable appears a Prince, who acts the part of an Executioner, and is made an Instrument by others to fulfil their cruel Designs against their Fellow Subjects? All Christian Princes therefore, as they tender their Consciences, ought to avoid all manner of Extreamities in Matters of this Nature, which ought never to be undertaken, unless they be well instructed beforehand in every particular Point. A Prince ought not only to be satisfyed with, or rely entirely on what is represented to him by his Clergy, (tho' never so pious in outward appearance;) there being too many Instances to be given, that the best of Princes, by their own Inclinations, abhorring all manner of Cruelty, have, by the Instigation of over-zealous Clergy-Men, turn'd the most cruel Tyrants: We scarce ever read of any Prince, who undertook to decide Controversies

Sovereigns in matters of Religion ought not to be misguided by Flatterers.

in Physick, or other Sciences (except he had attained to a particular Knowledge in these Matters) and, why should Sovereigns be too forward in deciding Religious Differences, which are of much greater Moment, (the eternal and temporal welfare of Millions of People do depend thereon) unless they be very well instructed in every thing that has any relation to it? And, since Princes very rarely bestow sufficient Time and Pains in being fully instructed in Divinity, it is to be wished, that they would be byassed by their own natural Understanding, rather than be influenc'd by the Opinions of others. As for an Instance, in those Controversies which are betwixt the *Protestants* and *Papists,* there are such evident Signs, from whence it is a difficult matter for a Christian Prince to discern, which of these two ought to be preferred before the other. For, if it be considered, that the *Protestants* are so far from forbidding the reading of the holy Scripture to the Laity, that on the contrary; they exhort them to it, and make the Scriptures the Touchstone of their Doctrine, and the true Judge of their Controversies; That the *Protestants,* trusting upon the goodness of their own Cause, do not forbid the reading of *Popish* Authors, but allow them to be publickly sold, as being confident, that the weakness of their Arguments cannot have any influence, even over an indifferent Understanding; it cannot but seem very strange, why in the Church of *Rome,* the Laity is not allowed the reading of the holy Scripture, nay, that they leave no stone unturn'd, to suppress the Validity of the holy Scripture; so, that in those places where the Inquisition is in vogue, a Man may with less danger be guilty of Blasphemy, Perjury, and other the most enormous Crimes, than to read and examine the Mysteries of the holy Scripture. On the other hand, what a clamour do they make about Traditions, and the Prerogatives of the Church, which Title they claim as belonging, in a most peculiar manner to themselves, and notwithstanding the same is not allowed them by others, they assume to themselves the Authority of giving Judgment in their own Cause. It is very well worth the Consideration of a Prince, that they will not allow our Books to be read among them, and especially, how careful they are in keeping them from the Knowledge of Great Men, tho' belonging to the Communion of their Church. Who is so ignorant as not to know, what great Difficulties and Obstacles were to be surmounted before it could be obtained, that the *Augsburgh* Confession was read to the Emperour *Charles* V. All which, taken together, are most evident Proofs to any unbyassed Person, that the *Protestants* act like Men, as relying upon the goodness of their Cause; but the *Roman Catholicks,* as mistrusting themselves, and fearing, that if their Doctrine should be examined, according to the Tenure of the holy Scripture, and out of the *Protestant* Writtings, the same would scarce bear the Touchstone. It may also be taken into consideration, how far different the Interest of the *Roman Catholicks* Party is from that of the *Protestants.* For, tho' both Parties with equal Zeal in Publick pretend to the Honour of God, and the Truth of the Gospel; and it is not to be denied, but that a great many among the *Roman Catholicks,* are very Zealous for the same; neverthe-less, if we duely consider the Nature of Mankind in general, it may easily be supposed, that they aim at something more; And, what this something is, is easily discernable, if we make a due comparison betwixt the Clergy of both Parties. Among the *Protestants,* the greatest part of the Clergy are so stinted in their Revenues, as to give them no oppor-tunity of living in State; what Respect is paid them, is on the account of their Function as being Teachers, their power very seldom reaches beyond their Revenues, which are very moderate, and oftentimes very mean. Both their Persons and Estates depend from the Authority of their Sovereigns, neither have they any where else to seek for Protec-tion. On the contrary, in what Pomp and affluence of Fortune does the *Popish* Clergy live! Unto what hight have they not exalted their Power in *Europe!* Have they not so ordered their Matters, as to be almost independant from the Civil Magistrates? What likelihood can there be in all this, that the *Protestants* should be as much concerned for a Temporal By-Interest as the *Popish* Clergy? For, whereas, they first can expect no more than what is alloted them already, the latter have no less in view than vast Riches, and the Possessions of whole King-doms. All these Matters duely considered, may be convincing Proofs, that all the Clamour which the *Popish* Clergy makes against the *Prot-*

estants, is of the same nature with that of *Demetrius* at *Ephesus,* when he exclaimed against St. *Paul,*[203] Love and Meekness being the products of the Christian Faith; the Cruelties of the *Popish* Clergy exercised against *Protestants,* ought to be suspected by Princes, and serve them as a forewarning; what good is to be expected from those that prosecute with so much Barbarity all such, as oppose their Pride and Ambition? After the Persecutions were ceased in the Primitive Church, the *Arians* were the first, who shew'd their teeth to the Christians; But they would have blushed for shame, if they should have attempted to propagate their Religion by force of Arms, and such other cruel Persecutions as are now in vogue among the *Popish* Clergy. If we were not sufficiently convinced, that the Spirit of Envy is not the Spirit of Christ; we may be instructed as to this Point by our Saviour himself (when he rebuked *James* and *John,* who would have fire come down from Heaven) in these words: *Ye know not, what manner of Spirit you are of; For the Son of Man is not come to destroy Mens lives, but to save them.*[204] The Sword of Christ is not girted on the side of Men, but goes out of his Mouth,[205] and in all the holy Scripture, there is not one passage, where the Church of Christ is said to be drunken with the Blood of Hereticks; but it is said of the Whore of *Babylon,* that *she is drunken with the Blood of the Saints, and with the Blood of the Martyrs of Christ.*[206]

§52. Lastly, Since Sovereigns ought to be jealous of their own Prerogatives, they may without Injustice make an Enquiry, whether the Protestant or the Popish Religion be most encroaching upon their Authority, and which of these two be most consistent with the Civil Government. For whenever the Civil Power bears any diminution under a Religious Pretence, it is then high time for Sovereigns to look about them, to examine upon what Foundation these Pretensions are built; it being evident, that Civil Government was introduced before

Marginal note: Sovereigns are often encroached upon in their rights under a religious pretext.

203. Acts 19:24, 25, 26, 27.
204. Luke 9:54, 55, 56.
205. Rev. 19:15.
206. Rev. 17:6.

the Christian Religion, and that therefore it ought plainly to be demonstrated, how Civil Authority came to be diminished by the Christian Religion. Now, if we look into the Constitution of the Popish Clergy, it is manifest, that by many steps and degrees, and by various Artifices and Intrigues; they have at last patch'd up a Potent State of their own; and that their Supream Head, for these many Ages past, is possess'd of great Territories, and Acts as a Sovereign; and, not only this, but also obtrudes his Authority upon all such as profess the *Roman* Catholick Religion. For, they don't think it sufficient that the whole Clergy have their dependance from him, but he pretends to an Absolute Authority of determining all Matters of Faith, by which means he is sure to guide the Minds of the People where ever he pleases. If any thing in the World is destructive to the Civil Powers, it must of necessity be this, when a Party inhabiting their Territories, disown their Jurisdiction and depending from a Foreign Power; deny the Authority of their Natural Prince over them, or at least acknowledge it no longer than they think it convenient. If Neighbouring States are commonly the most jealous of one another, must it not be look'd upon as a great Solecism of State, to permit such as depend from a Foreign Jurisdiction to abide in the Commonwealth? It is next door to take Foreign Garisons into our Forts, or to allow a Foreign Force to Encamp in the midst of our Dominions. And this Mischief seems to be the more pernicious, when the Revenues, by which the Grandeur of this Ecclesiastical State is maintained, are squeezed out of the Subjects of any Prince, and the best part of his Territories exhausted; whereas on the contrary, these Leeches are not only freed from all manner of Taxes, but also pretend to a Legislative Authority, so as to inflict Punishments upon the Subjects, and to Absolve them from their Allegiance due to their Sovereigns. I cannot see how Princes, without great Prejudice to the Commonweal, can allow the least Authority over their Persons, to the Clergy; For, if the Prince and they happen to jar together, the poor Subjects pay for it with a Vengeance, when they are to serve two Masters of a contrary side at one time; and the Taxes must fall the heavier upon the Subjects, where the Clergy are exempted from all Contributions. Lastly, is it not a heavy Burthen to the Subjects, to be subject both to an Ecclesiastical and Temporal Jurisdiction? The former being generally the most severe; as is most evident in *Spain* and *Italy,* where the Courts of Inquisition are in vogue. It being therefore beyond all question, that all these things are practised by the *Roman* Catholicks, but in no wise by the Protestants, such Princes, as, being misled by the Popish Clergy, endeavour to extirpate their Protestant Subjects, Act not only contrary to Justice, but even against the very Dictates of right Reason. What has been objected by some, *viz.* That Protestants have not been altogether free from the imputation of raising Disturbances in the State, and having joined with a Foreign Power, scarce deserves an Answer; For, this is not to be imputed to Religion it self, but rather, to some dangerous Juncture, and other Circumstances, which often prove the occasion of dangerous Commotions in a State; Or else, the Papists have first begun the Dance, and what Wonder is it, if some Protestants, to avoid their cruel Designs against them, have endeavoured to repel the Fury of their Adversaries; and when they found themselves insufficient, have sought for Aid by Foreign Princes. For, as it is the greatest piece of Injustice to compel Subjects by force of Arms to any Religion, so these may justly defend their Religion by force of Arms, especially if they live under a Government where they have a Right belonging to them of Protecting their Liberties against any Invaders.

Concerning the Right of Reformation. §53. Last of all, it very well deserves to make an Enquiry who it is that has the Power in the Commonwealth to amend such Errors and Abuses, as are crept into the Church, either in Point of Doctrine, Morality, or Church-Government? Or, which turns to the same Account, who has the Right of Reformation? Where first of all it is unquestionable, that there is no occasion of a Reformation, where the Clergy, upon Admonition, desist from these Abuses; like as when a Creditor, upon Summons, is paid by his Debtor, ought to supercede his Action against him. But, put the case, that the Clergy either absolutely refuse, or from time to time protract to desist from such Abuses, so that there is but two ways left to be chosen; either patiently to submit to their capricious Humour, or else certain Persons, in the

State, being damnified by these Abuses, have a Right and Power to controul their Extravagancies. Those that maintain the first Position, must prove, that the Clergy has been invested with such an unlimited Power by God Almighty, to impose upon Christians, even the most absurd Matters, at leasure, without being liable to be controuled by any Power upon Earth; Or, they must demonstrate, that Christians have absolutely submitted their Faith to the Clergy, and that in such a manner, that every thing which should be ordained by them, should be received for Truth with all imaginable submission and patience. But, because it would favour of too much Impudence to pretend to the first, it lies then at their Door to prove, that the Clergy, and their Supream Head, did never err, either in Point of Doctrine, Ceremonies, or Church-Government; All which having been sufficiently demonstrated to the contrary, by the consent of several Christian Nations. We are of Opinion, that when any Abuses are crept into the Church, which are prejudicial to the Commonwealth, or the Authority of Sovereigns, these, by vertue of their Sovereign Right and Prerogative, have a Power to abolish and reform all such matters as interfere with the Publick Good and Civil Authority. At the same time, it cannot be denied, but that in a case of such moment it may be very convenient to acquaint the People with the Reasons of such a Reformation, lest they should be surprized at it, and look upon it as an Innovation, which might prove of dangerous consequence. And, if especially, the Rights of the People are invaded by these Abuses, this Reformation ought to be undertaken with the knowledge and approbation of the Subjects. It may be objected, that by such a Reformation Divisions are raised in the Church. But this is to be look'd upon as a matter of no great Weight; such a Division being not to be imputed to those that rectifie such Errors, but to those that obstinately refuse to return into the right Path, either out of Self-interest or Pride. There is nothing more obvious out of the antient Ecclesiastical History, than that such as were plainly convicted of an Error, used to be excluded from the Communion of the Church. But such as begin a Reformation upon a good and legal Account, can under no Colour whatsoever be accused of Schism or Rebellion. For, those are Rebels, who by forcible Ways endeavour to withdraw themselves from the Allegiance due to their lawful Sovereign: Whereas all such as free themselves from Abuses unjustly imposed upon them, without their own consent, or any Divine Authority, rather deserve to be stiled defenders of their own Liberty and Conscience; especially, if these Abuses and Errors are dangerous to their Souls. For, no Teacher, no Bishop, no Convention whatsoever, was ever invested with an absolute Power of domineering over Christians at pleasure, so that no Remedy should be left against their Usurpation. It cannot therefore but be look'd upon as a great piece of Impudence in the *Roman Catholick* Party, when they assume to themselves wholly and entirely the Title of the Church, with exclusion to all others, that are not of the same Communion. For, they either must pretend their Church to be the Universal, or else a particular Church. By the Universal Church, is, according to the Tenure of the Holy Scripture, understood the whole multitude of the Believers, wheresoever dispersed in the World, whose Union consists in this, That they acknowledge one God, one Redeemer, one Baptism, one Faith and Eternal Salvation; from whence only are excluded such as pretend to dissolve this Union; that is, who deny the true God, and his Son Christ, and who do not agree with the very Fundamental Principles of the Christian Religion. This is the true Catholick Church, not the Pope with his Ecclesiasticks and Ceremonies, who impose their Authority upon Christendom. And, since those that, for weighty Reasons have withdrawn themselves from the Church of *Rome,* may and do believe a true Baptism, a true God and Father, a Faith agreeable to the Holy Scripture, it is evident that the *Roman* Church is not to be taken for the Universal Church; and that a Christian may be a Member of the true Catholick Church, in a right sense, notwithstanding that he never was in the Communion of the *Roman* Church, or, upon better Consideration, has freed himself from its Abuses and Errors. But the Popish Religion, considered as a particular Church, as it ought to be, (tho', if we unravel the bottom of its modern Constitution, it will easily appear, that the whole frame of that Church is not so much adapted to the Rules of a Christian Congregation, as to a Temporal State; where, under a Religious pretext, the chief aim is to extend its Sovereignty over the greatest part of

Europe) those, that have withdrawn themselves from that Communion, are no more to be counted Rebels, than our Modern Philosophers are to be taken for Fools and Madmen, because they differ in Opinion from *Aristotle*. For, all Believers, who adhere to the true Faith, are, in regard of their Head Jesus Christ, of an equal degree, and aim all at the same End. And Christ having given this Promise to all Believers; *That where two or three were gathered together in his Name, there would he be in the midst of them;*[207] no Church can claim any Prerogative by reason of the number of its Adherents. What the *Romanists*[208] alledge for themselves out of the Apostolical Creed, is so full of absurdity, that it contradicts it self, *viz.* out of these words: *I believe in one Holy, Catholick, and Apostolical Church;* For, except they could cajole us into a belief that these words imply as much as to say: There is but one true Church upon Earth, which is the *Roman Catholick,* there being no other besides that, I cannot see what Inference can be drawn from thence to their Advantage; Besides, that the very sense of the words contradict this Interpretation, if Reason, the Holy Scripture, and Experience it self did not sufficiently convince us to the contrary. It is beyond contradiction, that there is but one true Church upon Earth, there being but one God, one Christ, one Baptism, and one Faith; But, concerning one Point, many Errors and Abuses may be committed. Neither have the Popish Party any reason to brag of a particular Holiness, especially concerning these matters, wherein they differ from the Protestants. The word *Catholick,* relates here to a Doctrine, not to a Sovereign State, whose Authority is to be Universal over Christendom, so that that Church is to be esteemed a Catholick Church, which contains every particular Point of Doctrine in the true sense, as they are proposed in the Holy Scripture; And those are called Hereticks, who only profess some particular Points out of the Holy Writ, (for such as absolutely reject it, are counted Infidels and Reprobates) but either deny, or explain the rest in a wrong and perverted sense. How can the Popish Clergy therefore assume the Title of the Catholick

207. Matt. 18:20.
208. The Roman Catholics. [SZu]

Church, before they have, and that without contradiction, proved every Point of their Faith out of the Holy Scripture? Or, exclude us Protestants from that Title, till they have proved that our Doctrine is contrary to it? Lastly, It is called the Apostolical Church, as being founded upon the Doctrine of the Apostles. And the true Church loses nothing of its intrinsick Value, whether it has been planted by the Apostles, or whether the Apostolical Doctrine has been transmitted to them by others.

§54. But it is not a very difficult Task to introduce a Reformation in Religion with the mutual Consent of Sovereign and Subjects; so it may be questioned, whether Subjects may attempt a Reformation, when their Sovereigns, and the whole Clergy, or at least the greatest part of them, do not acknowledge their Error, but rather pretend to maintain it? In this case, it is our Opinion that, provided these Errors to touch the Fundamental Points of our Faith, such Subjects, as by the Grace of God, and the Light of his holy Spirit have attained the true Knowledge, may separate themselves from the Communion of that Church, without the consent of their Sovereigns or the Clergy. For, every body being accountable to God for his Religion, and answerable for his own Soul, whose Salvation cannot absolutely be committed to any Body else; and, a Christian, in Matters of Faith, being not altogether to rely upon his Sovereign or the Clergy, (at least no farther than their Doctrine is congruous with the holy Scripture.) It is undeniable, that Subjects may separate themselves from the Communion of that Church, which is professed by their Sovereign and Clergy, provided they can make it evidently appear, that such a Church is infected with gross Abuses, and dangerous Errors. For, the Church is a Colledge, whose Members are not kept in Union by any Temporal Power, but by the Union of the Faith; and, whosoever relinquishes that, he dissolves the sacred Tye of the Believers. Besides that, it is not absolutely necessary for our Salvation, that the Church be composed of a great Number, but the same may be obtained, either by a greater or lesser Number of the Believers. Neither can this Separation prove in the least prejudicial to the Sovereign Authority, it being supposed, that those who have

Whether Subjects, without the Consent of their Sovereigns, may separate themselves from an Erroneous Religion?

separated themselves adhere to the true pure Doctrine of the Gospel, free from all Poison, and Principles dangerous or prejudicial to the Government. For, civil Society was not instituted for Religion's sake; neither does the Church of Christ participate of the nature of a Temporal State; and therefore a Prince that embraces the Christian Faith, does not thereby acquire an absolute Sovereignty over the Church or Mens Consciences. So, that, if, notwithstanding this Separation, the Subjects pay due Allegiance to their Prince in Temporal Affairs, there is no reason sufficient which can oblige him to trouble them meerly upon the score of their Consciences. For, what loss is it to the Prince, whether his Subjects are of the same Religion with himself, or of another? Or, (which was supposed before) whether they did maintain the same Errors, as he does? The case indeed, would be quite different, if they should endeavour to withdraw themselves from their Allegiance, to set up a separate Society without his Consent; tho' it is undeniable, that there are some Cases of Necessity, when this civil Tye or Allegiance may be dissolved, as for Instance; when Subjects, for want of sufficient Protection from their natural Prince, are so hardly pressed upon by a more Potent Enemy, that they are forc'd to submit to his Power. And granted the Power of Sovereigns in the Church to be much greater, than in effect it is, Subjects are nevertheless bound to take care of their Souls, whose Salvation is to be preferr'd before all other things, in regard of which they may separate themselves from an Established Religion, provided they are convinced of its Errors. For, that Subject who sacrifices his Life for his Prince, does doubtless a glorious Action; but what Prince can be so unreasonable, as to expect that his Subjects should Sacrifice their Souls to the Devil for his sake. That Prince therefore who does trouble his faithful Subjects for no other reason, but because they cannot conform to his Opinion (especially if they can maintain theirs out of the Holy Scripture) commits an Act of Injustice; Nay, I cannot see how he can with Justice force them out of his Territories. It is true, he may refuse to receive Hereticks into his Dominions, unless it be for Reasons of State; Neither can a true Believer take it amiss, if he is not permitted to settle in a Commonwealth govern'd by Hereticks. For, the Right of Naturalization belongs to Sovereigns, which they may refuse and give to whom they think it convenient. But, as it is certainly the greatest Injustice in the World, to force an in-born Natural Subject, who has settled all his Fortunes in a Commonwealth, meerly for his Religion's sake, without being convicted of his Error, out of his Native Country, to the great detriment and danger of himself and his Family. So, if a Subject inclines voluntarily to leave his Native Country, either to avoid the Frowns of his Prince, or the hatred of the Clergy and Common People, and to serve God with more freedom according to his own Conscience, it ought not to be refused by his Sovereign. I remember there is a certain Proverb used among the *Germans,* viz. *He that Commands the Country, Commands Religion.* But this cannot be applied to the Princes of the *Roman Catholick* Religion, who cannot lay any Claim to it, it being evident that the Popish Clergy do not allow any such thing to these Princes; And, as to what concerns the Protestant Estates of *Germany,* it cannot be denied, but that they made use of this Pretension against the Emperor at the time of the Reformation, which however ought to be thus interpreted; That they denied the Emperor to have any Power of intermedling in the Affairs relating to their own Dominions, not, that only they claim'd it as belonging to the Rights of Sovereignty to impose any Religion, tho' never so false, upon their Subjects; notwithstanding all which, there are not wanting Examples, that Princes have acted conformable to this Proverb with their Subjects. A Prince, who troubles his faithful Subjects meerly upon the score of Religion, commits a gross Error; no Christian Prince being obliged to propagate his Religion by forcible means; provided his Subjects stand firm to their Allegiance to him, he being not answerable in particular for their Religion. It cannot be taken notice of without astonishment, how both in former times and our Age, some Princes, who were naturally not enclined to Cruelty, having in other respects given great Proofs of their Clemency, yet have been prevailed upon to raise the most horrid Persecutions against their Subjects, barely upon the score of Religion. But it has been foretold in Holy Scripture, that this Fate should attend the Christian Church, when it is said, That *Mighty Kings upon Earth should commit Whoredom with the Whore of Babylon.*[209] And, who is ignorant that Gallants will often commit the most barbarous Acts, meerly to please their Harlots? All true Christians therefore ought couragiously to oppose the Threats and Attempts of this Beast, committing the rest to Divine Providence. And, as for such Princes and States, as have shaken off the Yoke of Popish Slavery, if they seriously reflect, how their fellow-Protestants are persecuted, and in what barbarous manner they are treated, will, questionless without my Advice, take such measures, as may be most convenient for to secure themselves from so imminent a Danger.

209. Rev. 18:3.

The following
ANIMADVERSIONS
Made by the Author, upon some Passages of a Book, Entituled,
A POLITICAL EPITOMY,
Concerning the Power of Sovereigns in Ecclesiastical Affairs.

WRITTEN BY
ADRIAN HOUTUYN, [210]
Having a very near Relation to the former TREATISE,
it was thought fit to Insert them here by way of
APPENDIX

It is a Question of the greatest moment, which, if rightly determined,
tends to the Benefit of Mankind in general, *viz.* Unto whom, and under
what Limitations the Power in Ecclesiastical Affairs is to be ascribed
in the State? If the old Proverb, *That those who chuse the middle way
are commonly the most successful,* has not lost its force, it may without
question, be most properly applied in this Case, where both Extreams
are equally dangerous, since thereby the Consciences of Subjects are
left to the arbitrary disposal, either of the Pope of *Rome,* or their Sovereigns. There having not been wanting, both in the last and our Age,
Men eminent for their Learning, who have with very solid Arguments
opposed the Tyranny of the first, it is but reasonable for us, to take
heed, that since we have escaped the danger of *Scylla,* we may not be
swallowed up by *Charybdis.* For, as scarce any body that is in his right
Senses can go about to deny, that the Sovereign Power ows its original
either to God, or the general Consent of the People; So it is a matter

210. See section V of the editor's introduction. [SZu]

mutually advantageous both to the Prince and Subjects, to understand, how far this Power is limited in the State, that the first may not transgress their due Bounds, and, instead of being Fathers of their Subjects, prove their most dangerous Enemies. *Adrian Houtuyn,* a Civilian in *Holland,* having in a Treatise, called *A Political Epitomy,* inserted several Assertions tending to the latter of these two Extremes, and it having been observed of late, that this Book has been recommended by some *Doctors* in the Law, to the great detriment of young Students; I thought it not amiss to make some Animadversions upon his LXIII, and following SECTIONS, which may serve as a Guide to the younger Sort, lest they, under the Cloak of asserting the Prerogatives of Sovereigns, may be mislead into the latter of these Extremes, and attribute that to the Prince, which God has reserved as his own Prerogative, and thus, irrecoverably, play the Prodigal with their own Liberty and Property.

This Author speaking concerning the Prerogative of Princes, *Sect.* LXIII, runs on thus: *He has an uncontroul'd Power over all External, Ecclesiastical Affairs, which are not determined in the Holy Scripture.* He alledges for a Reason, because that Power is granted to Sovereigns at the same time when Subjects submitted themselves and their Fortunes to their Disposal. But it ought to be taken into Consideration, that certain Matters belonging to the external Exercise of Religious Worship have so strict an Union with the internal Part, that, if the first be not disposed in a manner agreeable to this inseparable Tye, the latter must of necessity undergo such Alterations, as are inconsistent with its Nature. And, since Mr. *Houtuyn* do's not leave the internal Part to the Disposal of Sovereigns, how can the exterior Worship be submitted to their meer Pleasure, considering this strict Union betwixt them? Besides this *General Submission,* he admits of Limitation, in regard of that End, for which Civil Societies were Instituted, which is, the mutual defence against Violences: From whence it is evident, that there are certain Matters, belonging to every private Person, derived from the State of natural Freedom, which were not absolutely left to the Disposal of Sovereigns, at least, no further than they were necessary to obtain that End. Religion having not any relation to this End, it is not to be imagined, that Subjects did submit their Religion to the arbitrary

Pleasure of Sovereigns. And, it being unquestionable, that Subjects may exercise certain Acts belonging to them by Vertue of an inherent Right, derived from the free State of Nature, and independent from their Sovereigns, it may rationally be concluded, that, when Subjects did submit themselves, in Matters of Religion, to their Sovereigns, it was done with this Supposition, that both the Prince and Subjects were of one and the same Religion; and that the external Exercise of Religious Worship was not left to the Disposal of the first, any further, than in such Matters as are indifferent in regard of the internal Part of it. What is alledged concerning the *maintaining a good Order, and avoiding of Confusion,* it is to be observed, that this is not the main End, for which Civil Societies were Instituted, nor has it any relation to it, but only thus far, as it may be instrumental to maintain the Publick Tranquility.

As to *N.* 2. It is to be observed, that, because Priests have a dependance from the Civil Power in certain Respects belonging to its Jurisdiction, this does not involve Religion (considered as such) under the same Subjection. The following words ought also to be taken notice of: *A Christian Prince commands over the Church, as being a Colledge, and representing one single Person in the Commonwealth. The Church, thus considered, is a Civil Society or Body Politick, founded upon the Publick Authority and Power, and ought to be regarded, as being in the same condition with other Colledges and Bodies Politick; and in this Sense a King is the Head of the Church in his Dominions.* Whoever will consider the real difference betwixt the Church and Commonwealth, must needs find as many Errors, as there are words here. For, because a Prince has the Sovereign Jurisdiction in a Commonwealth, consisting of Christian Subjects; no inference is to be made, that therefore he may, in the same degree, exercise his Sovereignty in the Church, as in the Commonwealth, and that in the same Sense, he may be called, *The Supream Head of the Church, as of the Commonwealth.* 'Tis true, the Church is a Society, but not a Body Politick, founded upon the Publick Authority, but owes its Original to a higher Principle, having not, like other Colledges, its dependency from the State, What is alledged out of *Titus,* 2:9. *Colos.* 3:20, 22. *Rom.* 13:3, 4. 1 *Pet.* 2:14. is strangely misrepresented to evince, that Ecclesiastical Matters are dependent from the absolute Pleasure of Sovereigns. What Follows might also very well deserve some Animadversions, if it were not beyond our scope at present.

N. 13. It is a gross Error, That, *as a Consequence of this Sovereign Power in Ecclesiastical Affairs,* he attributes to them, *the Titles of Pastors, Ministers, Heralds of God, Bishops, Priests, and Apostles.* Pray, with what Authority, and with what sense? For, the Duty belonging to Sovereigns, which entitles them to the name of *being the Guardians of both Tables of the Decalogue, and of being the Foster-Fathers and Defenders of the Church,* is of a far different Nature from what he would insinuate here. And, if it be not to be left to the absolute Judgment of the Clergy it self, with exclusion of the rest of the Members of the Church, to determine in Ecclesiastical Affairs, what is agreeable to the Word of God, how can this Judgment belong to the Sovereign alone, without allowing a share to the rest of the Members of the Church?

These words in the §. LXIV. *Each Sovereign may establish what Religion he pleases in his Dominions,* ought not to be let pass by without a severe Correction. The Reason alledged is very frivolous: *Because all Publick and external Actions depend from the Publick Authority.* Is this your Assertion, good Mr. *Houtuyn,* that Princes may impose what Religion they please upon their Subjects, and by their absolute Authority make it the establish'd Religion, with exclusion to all others, who, if not complying, must, forsooth, fly the Country? What Religion they please, do you say! the Pagan, False, Fictious, or Superstitious, it matters not which. From whence, pray, was this Power derived to Sovereigns? Not certainly from God, except you can shew us a Divine Authority for it. Not from the common consent of those that entred into Civil Societies; Commonwealths not being instituted for Religion's sake, and of a later date; besides, that such a Power is not requisite for the attaining that end, for which Civil Societies were establish'd. Neither is it left to the bare pleasure of any Person, tho' considered as in the Natural state of Freedom, to profess what Religion he pleases: But, supposing it was, no Inference can be made from thence, that the same may be forc'd upon others. The distinction he makes betwixt the *internal and external Religion,* must also be taken with a great deal of

Circumspection, lest some People might perswade themselves, that it is indifferent what Religion a Man professes in outward shew, provided he be satisfied as to the internal part of it. Furthermore, it is absolutely false, that all Publick Actions, that is, every thing done in Publick in the Commonwealth, owes its Original to the Sovereign Power; there being several things to be done by Subjects in publick, depending meerly from that Liberty belonging to them in the Natural state of Liberty, or from God's Command, or from a certain Power granted to them by God Almighty.

It is no less false, That all exterior Actions depend from the Civil Authority; For, according to Mr. *Houtuyn's* Opinion, the Doctrine of Divinity, and the Confession of Faith, as comprehended in a certain form, are to be reckoned among those exterior Actions. Mr. *Houtuyn* is much in the wrong, when he pretends to draw an Inference from thence; that, because it belongs to Sovereigns to take care, that their Subjects may be well instructed concerning what Opinion they ought to have of God, as the Establisher of Justice; they therefore have a Right of disposing (in an Arbitrary way) of revealed Religion, and to declare any Religion whatsoever, which pretends to Revelation, the Establish'd Religion in the Commonwealth. It is a much grosser Mistake yet, when he asserts: That *any Religion establish'd in a State, tho' never so false, contributes to the Publick Tranquility of that Commonwealth.* It is possible that a Religion defective in some Points, may nevertheless lead People into the way of Salvation; but those that contain false Doctrines of God and his Attributes, are incapable of producing that Effect. The Publick Tranquility, founded upon such false Opinions, will be very unstable, and may with more ease, or at least with the same conveniency be obtained by the true Doctrine; especially if it be taken into consideration, that, tho' it be possible that such Impostures may beguile the giddy-headed Multitude, they cannot always pass for currant among Men of a sound Understanding: It is to be remembred, that the Southsayers at *Rome* cannot forbear laughing, when they meet another of the same Profession. We must beg Mr. *Houtuyn's* Pardon, if we question his Authority, when he pretends to perswade us: That *Faith,* which he is pleased to call *every ones private*

Religion, independent from any Temporal Power, will not be impaired by a Man's professing any other Religion, established by the Sovereign Authority; and he leaves it to the discretion of those Civil Governours, which of all Religions they will be pleased to establish in their Dominions, whether that of the *Japoneses,* of the *Brachmans, Mahometans, Jews,* or *Christians;* and among all those that pretend to the Christian Name, such a one as may be most agreeable to their own Fancy. I much question, whether he will meet with many Tools, that will take his Word for it. A great part of Christendom did look upon it as a thing insufferable, that the Pope of *Rome* should set up for the great Arbitrator of Christendom in matters relating to the Christian Faith, tho' his Pretences did not reach further than to force one Religion upon the World, which he knew was most likely to turn to his own Advantage: But now it seems it has pleased God, that Sovereigns should be invested with a Power of establishing any Religion at pleasure; and it being beyond question, that there are several Religions which have not the least relation to one another, they may, with the same Right, at several times, declare, several distinct Religions, nay, even those that are quite opposite to one another, the establish'd Religion, and nevertheless every one of these must be accepted, forsooth, as the true Religion. The next Consequence will be, that Sovereigns, having a Right of defending and altering the establish'd Religion, and to punish such as trespass against it, one Prince will have no more Right to cherish and maintain one Religion, but his Successors may, with the same Right, abolish it, and punish such of his Subjects as adhere to it. So that according to the Doctrine of Mr. *Houtuyn's* Gospel, the establish'd Religion will be settled upon the same Foundation with some Statutes, which may be enacted and repeal'd by Sovereigns at pleasure.

In §. LXV. He entirely, and without limitation, ascribes to the Prince the Power of *Constituting Ministers of the Gospel, in the same manner as if they were Ministers of the State.* But in the Commonwealth of the *Jews,* regulated according to God's own Institution, no such Power was granted to their Kings; Neither had the Apostles themselves, tho' the most general Teachers that ever were (as being sent to Preach the Gospel to all the World) their Authority of Teaching from any Temporal Sovereigns. Neither can it be proved, that the Church, at the time, when Sovereigns first embraced the Christian Faith, did transfer this Power of constituting Ministers of the Gospel, without limitation, to those Princes; tho' at the same time it is not to be denied, but that Sovereigns have a considerable share in it. His Argument taken from *the care Parents ought to have of the Salvation of their Children,* does not reach to what he pretends to prove; for, says he, Princes being the Publick Fathers of the Commonwealth; *it belongs to their Princely Office, to provide for the Eternal Salvation of their Subjects.* For, besides that, the Title of *Father of the Commonwealth* is a Metaphorical Expression, the Fatherly and the Regal Office depend from a quite different Principle, and the care to be taken of Children of a tender Age, is of another Nature with that which ought to be employed for the Safety of a whole People; neither were Sovereigns invested with the Supream Authority to enable them to procure Eternal Salvation to their Subjects, God having prescribed other ways and means for the obtaining of it. It cannot be denied, but that a Prince must not be regardless of this Care, nevertheless ought the same not to reach beyond its due Bounds, but must be effected by such Methods as are approved of in the Holy Scripture, and suit with the true Genius of the Christian Religion; Wherefore, it is in vain to attribute to Sovereigns a Power of obtruding any Religion, at pleasure, upon their Subjects; it being beyond question, that not all Religions are conducing to obtain Eternal Salvation. So *Abraham,* the Father of Believers, did not impose upon his Children what Religion he thought most convenient, but he charged them to walk in the ways of the Lord, such as were manifested to them in the Holy Scripture. What St. *Paul* says, I *Tim.* 2:2. is very well worth taking notice of, *viz.* That the chief care of the Supream Governours shall be, so to Rule over their Subjects, that they may live under them, not only honestly, but piously; this being the way to Eternal Salvation. It is to be observed, that those Princes, for whom the Apostle enjoined the Christians to pray, being Pagans, made but little account of Piety, especially of that belonging to the Christians; but it was thought sufficient for the Christians to enjoy the common Benefit of the Publick Tranquility under their Protection, the rest being left to their own care.

So we read that the Poet's enjoyment of his Muses, was owing to *Augustus Caesar's* Protection; nevertheless the Emperor did not concern himself about the Rules of Poetry. Furthermore, it is a very gross way of Arguing, when he Asserts: That, *the Commonwealth and Church are both one and the same thing under a Christian Prince, whose Subjects also profess the Christian Religion, the only difference being in respect of their different Qualifications: They being in the Commonwealth to be considered as they are Subjects, in the Church as Believers.* It seems, Mr. *Houtuyn* looks upon that Difference to be of little moment, which arises from divers Moral Qualifications, and includes different Obligations, and is founded upon another Legal Principle. It is confess'd, that in such a case where the Head is not differing in his Natural Constitution from the Rights and Power belonging to him, the rest of the Members, tho' differently considered under divers Qualifications, are nevertheless to be look'd upon as one and the same Society. As for instance: If a Prince puts himself at the Head of all his Subjects upon an Expedition, these, tho' they may be considered either as Soldiers or Subjects, yet do not differ in any Essential Part; As for Example: The People of *Israel,* when going upon their Expedition under the Conduct of *Joshua,* was the very same that afterwards, under his Protection, enjoyed and inhabited the Country of *Canaan.* But the Church and Commonwealth, tho' composed out of the self-same Persons, do not only differ in their very Foundation, but also a Sovereign cannot claim the same Right and Name of being the Supream Head of the Church in the same sense, as he is the Supream Governour of the State. For, in the latter he exercises his Authority without controul, being subject to no body; But, the Head of the Church is Christ, who Rules it by his Word, announced to us by the Teachers of the Church; so, that a Sovereign cannot as much as claim the Right of being Christ's Vicegerent in the Church; And, on the other hand, tho' it is said of Christ, *That all Power is given unto him in Heaven, and upon Earth,*[211] nevertheless it cannot be said of him, to be, in the same manner, the Head of Civil

211. Matt. 16:19.

Societies, as of the Church. The next following Assertion runs thus: *Where the whole Commonwealth is not composed out of Christians, the Church is a Congregation of the Believers in the Commonwealth.* But, where all Subjects are Christians, the Church is nevertheless nothing else than a Colledge in the Commonwealth. But what he alledges of the Church being sometimes taken in the same sense with the Commonwealth, is absolutely false. For the words, κατ᾽ ἐκκλησίαν in *Acts* 14:23. and those in *Titus* 1:5. κατα πόλιν are no Synonyms; but the latter is to be understood thus: In all the Towns and Cities, where there was any Christian Church. The Inference he would make from the Military Function, and the Administration of Justice, being both included in one Government, is to no purpose; both of them owing their Offspring to that End for which Civil Societies were instituted, which is not the same in the Church; and Sovereigns are entrusted with the Sword of War and Justice, not with the Ministerial Function of Preaching the Gospel. From whence it comes, that Generals and Judges are subordinate to the Princely Office, but not the Ministers of the Gospel, they being (barely considered as such) not properly Ministers of the Prince and State, but Ministers of Christ and the Church. He says further; *That the assignation of the Ministerial Function does not appertain to the Internal part of Religion.* But if Faith comes from hearing, and no body can believe, without being instructed; it is undeniable, that those that Preach the Gospel, have a share in the internal part of Religion, they being considered as the Instruments, by the help of whom, the Gospel, and consequently the Faith, is conveyed to their Auditors. It is false, when he asserts, That Sovereigns, tho' no Christians, have a Right of constituting Ministers; *For,* says he, *their Right is the same.* But a Prince, who makes not Profession of the Christian Faith, tho' he has Christian Subjects under his Jurisdiction, and allows them the free Exercise of their Religion, has nevertheless not the least Power over their Church, as being no Member of it. It is no less false, what he says, that since Princes are become Christians, the Vocation of Ministers does no more depend from the Church; *Just as a Man, by submitting himself under another Jurisdiction, is no more at his own disposal.* For, a Prince by becoming a Member of the Church, does thereby not make himself Master of that Church, but rather submits to the Obedience of Christ, the Head of the Church; and therefore does not incroach all its Rights to himself, but only can claim his share as such, unless a certain Church should voluntarily surrender its Rights, as far as it lies in its power, to the Sovereign. And I see no reason, why the Church may not be under the Protection of a Christian Sovereign, *as representing a certain Person in the Commonwealth; and therefore to Act and Decree by plurality of Votes, which implies a Right, at least by Consent.* For, there is a *Medium* betwixt the State or Commonwealth and a disorderly Multitude, *viz.* a Colledge, where there is no occasion for a coercive Sovereign Power. This may be illustrated by an Example: For, supposing in a Commonwealth a certain Society or Company of Merchants, regulated by certain Statutes of their own, under the Direction of some of its own Members. Into this Colledge a Prince has a mind to be received as a Member, paying his certain share. By being thus made a Member of this Company, he has not obtained an absolute disposal over this Society; but rather has accommodated himself to the Statutes of the Colledge, neither can he claim any other Prerogative there, but what is derived either from his share in that Company, or from a free Gift, and voluntary consent of the rest of its Members; and as a Member of this Colledge he is to be considered, not as a Prince, but as a Merchant. There is nevertheless one remarkable difference, *viz.* That it is in the Power of a Sovereign to hinder the setting up of such a Society, which is not the same in regard of the Church. He plainly betrays his Ignorance, when he says; *That the Church is to be considered as a multitude of People, comprehended in the Person of one Prince; from whence the Prince represents the People, like one Publick Person, through whom the whole People declare their Sentiments.* For, tho' this be appliable to the Commonwealth, it is not to the Church, they being quite different from one another. It cannot be denied, but that those who have the Sovereign Power in the State, may Enact what Laws they think most convenient; But to attribute the same Power to Sovereigns over the Church, is a Madness, and savours of Blasphemy. And, supposing a Prince should be misled into Errors, or Heresie, must therefore the whole Church be accounted Erroneous, or Heretical?

Except he would perswade us also, that Princes are Infallible. Wherefore in those places where the Election of Ministers is independent from the Prince, it is supposed to proceed from a Right transferred unto him by the Church; The same is to be understood, where this Election is managed either by the Bishops or Presbyters. But in case the same be done by the whole Church, it would be preposterous to say, that such an Election was made by vertue of a Priviledge granted by the Prince. Mr. *Houtuyn* having granted before, *That the Pastoral Function, not being annexed to any certain Person, (considered as such) had no dependency from the Civil Jurisdiction, but owed its Institution to Christ.* Nevertheless in §. LXVI. he affirms: *That the actual Administration of the Ministerial Function is an External Publick Act, such as is subject to the Civil Power.* Which is the same in effect, as if he said, Matrimony is a Divine Institution, but it depends from the Prince, whether he will allow his Subjects to Marry actually or not. For, supposing a Sovereign should take a Resolution to forbid the antient Exercise of the Ministerial Function, what would, in such a Case, become of this Pastoral or Ministerial Function? It is also insufferable what he says immediately after: *An Election is a voluntary Act, therefore revocable at pleasure;* it being certain, that it cannot be done without impairing the Reputation of the Minister.

What relates to §. LXVII. It is denied, that *Nebuchadonosor had any legal Authority* to put to Death such as refused to adore the great Statue, set up by his Order. For, a Prince who inflicts any Punishment upon his Subjects, against the express Command of the holy Scripture, does not, at that time exercise his legal Authority, but commits an hostile and tyrannical Act. So, when King *Ahab,* under pretence of a legal Process, and by subborning of false Witnesses,[212] possess'd himself of *Naboth*'s Vineyard, did no more exercise his legal Jurisdiction, than a Guardian may be said to do, when he commits a Rape upon a Pupil committed to his Management. But, when the same *Nebuchadonosor* publishes his Edict, *That no body dare to blaspheme the God of the Jews,*

212. 1 Kgs. 21:2ff.

he did, without all question, nothing but what belong'd to his high Station. He runs on further; *viz.* That *Peter, John, Stephen, Paul,* nay, even our Saviour himself, did appear before the *Sanhedrim,* before *Felix, Festus, Caesar* and *Pilate,* without taking the least Exception against the legality of their Jurisdiction. What could be more falsely invented? Did *Peter* and *John* acknowledge the Jurisdiction of the *Sanhedrim* in respect of the Christian Doctrine, when they told them to their very Faces, that they would not obey their Command, of not preaching in the Name of Jesus?[213] Did *Stephen* acknowledge the Jurisdiction of the *Sanhedrim,* when he told them, You uncircumcised in your Hearts and Ears, you always resist the holy Ghost? Neither is it an Argument, that *Paul,* and an infinite Number of Martyrs did acknowledge the Jurisdiction of those Princes, and other Civil Magistrates, when they, being forced to appear before them, endeavoured to prove their Innocence, there being no other Tribunal to which they could appeal; and it being at that time look'd upon as a Crime deserving Death, for any one to profess himself a Christian. All the defence they made may be reduced under two Heads: For they either denied those Crimes laid to their Charge, as calumnious, or else they asserted even to the last, That the profession of the Christian Religion did not depend from the Civil Jurisdiction. And those Magistrates that absolved the Confessors of this Truth, did in effect give this Sentence: *That this was a Cause not belonging to their Jurisdiction.* It is a wonder to me how Mr. *Houtuyn,* who pretends to be a Lawyer, can find out any thing in the least resembling a legal Process in that Action of *Pilate,* it being to be considered no otherwise than a publick Robbery, and *a power of darkness,*[214] since in all his Proceedings, there is not a footstep of a legal Process to be met with. And it is so manifest, that, when religious Matters were in question, the due Method and judicial Order of a legal Process have been violated a thousand times over and over, that it would be superfluous to alledge any Examples of it here. When Sovereigns punish or chastise a Pastor or Minister of the Church, who

213. Acts 4:19, 20.
214. Luke 22:53.

has abused his Function, or been defective in it, this power does properly not proceed from the Civil Jurisdiction, but from a Right translated to the Sovereign by the Church. But those that are punished by the Civil Authority, because *they have stirr'd up, by their turbulent Speeches and Sermons, the People to Rebellion against their Sovereigns, or have attempted to withdraw the Auditors from, and to resist the Power of a legal jurisdiction,* cannot be said to undergo Punishment on the account of the Christian Religion. Furthermore, it is false, that the Church (considered as such) can claim any Jurisdiction, properly speaking. It is no less false, that the Power of disposing and exercising those Functions, belonging to each Church, is a civil Act, in regard of its publick Effect. Mr. *Houtuyn* has been drawn into all these Errors, by confounding the Commonwealth with the Church. If these two be not very nicely distinguished, but we allow the Church to be entirely swallowed up in the civil Power, what have we got by shaking off the Popish Yoak? For, the condition of the Church will be never the better, if all Ecclesiastical Matters, without Exception are left to the arbitrary Disposal of Sovereigns; To maintain which, Mr. *Houtuyn,* in contradiction to all Reason and the Scripture it self, has invented; *A spiritual Good, or the eternal Welfare of People, as the main End and Duty of the Sovereign Power;* By Vertue of which, he enables his Prince to force his Subjects to profess publickly what Religion he will be pleased to impose upon them; tho' never so contrary to their own Opinion. For it may be sufferable for a Man to keep his own Opinion concealed to himself, but to be oblig'd to profess what is quite contrary to it, is both abominable and intolerable. The Saying of *Constantine the Great,* so much extoll'd by Mr. *Houtuyn* himself, is contradictory to his Assertion, *viz. That he could have wish'd, all his Subjects to have been Christians, but that he never forced any.* For, this Emperour not only never attempted to force any one from his own Opinion (which indeed was beyond his Power) but also never constrained his Subjects to profess themselves Christians against their own Inclinations. Our Author does also not a little contradict himself, in what he says concerning Words, sometimes exempting them from any civil Cognisance; whereas, before he had made them liable to the civil Jurisdiction: *What,* says he; *if our Faith express'd by Words should come to the knowledge of our Sovereign? It ought to be look'd upon not so much as a Crime, but rather as an Error, to correct which, is not to be effected by Punishments (which do illuminate our Mind) but rather by good Instructions.* But those that know the real difference betwixt the Commonwealth and Church, that is to say, betwixt the State and a Colledge, may without much difficulty dissolve these knotty Questions, which he has started concerning the Jurisdiction and Legislative Power of Princes over the Church.

As to the §. LXIX. It is to be observed, that it is put beyond all question, that Sovereigns have a Right to give the Authority and Force of a Law to such Statutes as they find suitable to the State, it being their Prerogative to determine, according to what Laws Judgment is to be given in Civil Courts of Judicature, what is punishable, and what is to be left to the Conscience of every Subject. But it implies in Absurdity, to attribute to Sovereigns a Right of giving publick Authority to Prophesies themselves, neither the Intrinsick nor Historical Faith having any dependence on the Civil Jurisdiction, by the force of which Subjects may be obliged to act, but not to believe. From whence it is evident, that if any Prophecy appear to be from God, it cannot receive any Addition by the Authority of the Prince, no more than if he should declare *Cicero* to be a good *Latin* Author. But in case a pretended Prophecy be either ambiguous or suppositious in it self, and a Prince should persuade himself to be able by his own Authority to make it pass current for Truth, he would be look'd upon as one beyond his Senses; What he insinuates concerning the New Testament in general, is much of the same Stamp: *It was not,* says he, *in the power of Christ and his Apostles, to establish this Doctrine* (of the New Testament) *by Publick Authority, which was the reason it remain'd in a private condition, till such time when Princes having received the Christian Faith, they gave it a publick Authority, and the force of Laws.* But the Rules and Doctrine of Christ cannot receive any additional Strength from the Civil Power, it being contrary to its Genius to be established and promoted by civil Punishments; For, whosoever out of fear of Temporal Punishments, professes in outward shew only this Doctrine, does not act according to, nor fulfil the Will of Christ.

The same may be reply'd to §. LXX. For, as the Scripture and the Christian Doctrine do not owe their Authority to the civil Jurisdiction, the latter being introduced in the Government by God's peculiar Assistance, in spite of all the Resistance of the civil Powers; So ought the Interpretation of the ambiguous and controverted Passages in the holy Scripture, not to be determined by the Sovereign Authority; it belonging not to the Prince only, but to the whole Church, or such as are authorised by the Church; tho' at the same time, the Prince, considered as the Chief Member of it, cannot be excluded from having his share in such a Debate. Is it a prophane Expression when he says: *Christ himself having an unquestionable Power of introducing a new Law, must needs have a right to interpret the same. But, since during the time of his abode here, he lived among those, that either out of Ignorance or Disobedience did not own Christ, and that in a private Condition, subject to the civil Power; it is evident, that his Laws, Doctrine, and the Interpretation of them, did acquire their obliging Power, and publick Authority from the civil Constitution.* A little more would have made the Office of Christ, as being Mediator of the World, also dependent from the civil Jurisdiction. It is not a prodigious Absurdity to affirm; *That the Doctrine of Christ has received its publick Authority from the civil Power, among those, who denied Christ? And what follows: That, if at the time of Christ, Princes had been Christians, they would have acknowledged him for the true God, and the Son of God, submitting themselves to his Judgment; so, that the Interpretation of the Christian Doctrine would have been owing by Christ, to their Submission.* Away with such Fictions not aggreeable even to common Sense. He might as well say, that God's Power over us Mortals did owe its original to the submission of Princes; and in case they thought fit to withdraw themselves from this Obedience, God Almighty (I cannot relate it without horror) must thereby be reduced to the Condition of a private Person.

In the next Assertion, he is not altogether so much beyond his Senses when he grants, even to Pagan Princes, a Right of determining the controverted Points among Christians, which is as much as to make a blind Man a competent Judge of the difference of Colours. When the Primitive Christians were forced to appear before the Pagan Judges, it was not on the Account of the Interpretation of the Scripture; The Christians could never be guilty of so gross an Error, as to Consult with the Unbelieving concerning the controverted Articles of Faith; But, being forced, against their will, to appear before them, they could not avoid to receive their Judgment, such as they were pleased to give, as having no way left them to decline it. Furthermore, our Author is pleased to affirm, That such an Interpretation ought to be look'd upon as establish'd by Publick Authority, which carries along with it an obliging force, at least in outward appearance; so, that Subjects are obliged to conform themselves to it by a verbal Confession, tho' never so discrepant, from that Opinion, they keep concealed within their hearts. But; the outward Behaviour, and verbal Confessions of a Christian, which are not aggreeable to the true Sentiments of his Heart, having not the least affinity with Religion it self, I don't see, upon what Account this Chimerical Power is attributed to Princes, unless it be, to furnish them with a specious pretext to afflict their Innocent Subjects. Thus much is certain, that Christ did not command his Doctrine to be propagated by forcible means; so that, supposing the Articles, thus established by the Civil Authority, to be never so consonant to Truth, it is nevertheless inconsistent with the Genius of the Christian Religion, to impose them upon Subjects by force, and under severe Penalties; But, supposing them to be false, the case of Subjects must needs be very miserable, when they suffer Punishment, because they will not profess an erroneous or false Doctrine. I see no other benefit to be reap'd from the egregious Assertions of our Author, than to serve for a Justification of the most Tyrannical Persecutions that have been, and to declare them to have been done by Vertue of a Legal Authority. At this rate it will be no difficult Task to justifie the Proceedings against the Protestants in *France,* which move both Pity and Horror in all good Men, at least, Mr. *Houtuyn* has very freely offered his Advice and Patronage. What follows next, is very smartly said, to wit, *That the Coercive Power may be Legal, whereas the Act of Obedience is not allowable.* No body of common sense but will acknowledge, that this implies a most manifest Contradiction, and, that the Legal Sovereign Authority, and the Obligation of paying Obedience to it, are inseparable from one another. Yet with this Nicety Mr. *Houtuyn* is so mightily taken, that he does not consider, that at the same time, he grants an absolute Authority to his Prince, to persecute his Subjects on the Account of Religion, he takes away from them the Power of denying the true Religion. But, what Reason can be given, why the one should have a coersive Power, where the other cannot obey; unless it be done on purpose to encourage ambitious and imperious Princes, either to force their Subjects to a sinful compliance, or never to want an Opportunity of afflicting the Innocent at Pleasure? For those that take to these violent ways of propagating the Faith, or rather (to speak Truth) Hypocrisie and Superstition, by their booted Apostles, are not contented to silence their Subjects, dissenting from them in Point of Religion, who are also debarr'd even to save themselves by flight; (tho' it be no small Misfortune to a Subject, to be forced to leave his Native Country) but they compel them to profess publickly those things for Truth, which they abhor in their Hearts, and appear to be Idolatrous, Superstitious, or Fictitious; invented on purpose by those that make their Market by Religion. Mr. *Houtuyn* himself cannot but confess, *That no body can safely acquiesce in any determination made concerning all Articles of Faith, unless by his own private Judgment he find it aggreeable to the Word of God. And, if he find it not consonant to that, he ought not to rest satisfied in it, for fear he should disown his Faith this being the worst and most unbecoming thing belonging to a Christian.* But, if it be unbecoming a Christian to deny his faith, which is the same in effect, *as to rest satisfied in one's own private Opinion and Conscience, to keep secret within the heart what one believes, not to indulge one's Tongue, and to refrain from External Actions.*

This being the Advice (which in contradiction to himself he had not long before given to the Dissenting Subjects) what Reason can he give for his Assertion; when he attributes to his Prince a Power so unlimited that his Christian Subjects must either be forced to undergo such an indignity, or else the most horrible Persecutions that can be invented? The first Inventer of this unlimited Power, as far as ever I could learn, was Mr. *Thomas Hobbs,* the worst Interpreter that ever was in Divinity; whose Opinion, as to this kind, no body has taken so much pains to revive with the same Impudence, as Mr. *Adrian Houtuyn.* What I most admire at, is, that this should be attempted by one living in a State, whose Maxims are quite opposite to these Principles, and where consequently he could not reasonably propose to himself any Reward of his Adulation; There being not the least likelihood that the States General of the *United Provinces* should ever lay claim to such Power; As it is not very probable that Princes will apply themselves to the Ministry of the Church and undertake the Publick Exercise of the Pastoral Function in Person; so that I cannot see to what purpose our Author has been so careful in asserting it, in the behalf of Sovereigns; Unless he has pleased himself with this Fancy, that his Assertions cannot fail to make him to be the more admired among the Youngsters, by how much the more remote they are from common Sense. Thus much at present for Mr. *Houtuyn.*

FINIS.

SELECTED BIBLIOGRAPHY

Selected Works by Samuel Pufendorf with the Titles under Which They Appeared in English

De statu imperii Germanici (*The Present State of Germany*), by Severinus de Monzambano (Pufendorf). 1667.

De jure naturae et gentium libri octo (*The Law of Nature and Nations*). 1672.

De officio hominis et civis juxta legem naturalem libri duo (*The Whole Duty of Man According to the Law of Nature*). 1673.

Basilii Hyperetae [Pufendorf's] *Historische und politische Beschreibung der geistlichen Monarchie des Stuhls zu Rom* (A Historical and Political Description of the Spiritual Monarchy of Rome [never translated into English]). 1679. Later included in the following work.

Einleitung zu der Historie der vornehmsten Reiche und Staaten so itziger Zeit in Europa sich befinden (*An Introduction to the History of the Principal Kingdoms and States of Europe*). 1682–86.

De habitu religionis christianae ad vitam civilem (*Of the Nature and Qualification of Religion in Reference to Civil Society*). 1687.

Jus feciale divinum sive de consensu et dissensu protestantium exercitatio posthuma (*The Divine Feudal Law: Or, Covenants with Mankind, Represented*). 1695.

Studies Related to *Of the Nature and Qualification of Religion in Reference to Civil Society*

Blumgart, Alice. *Pufendorfs Toleranzbegriff im Zusammenhang mit seinem Staatsbegriff.* Dissertation. Munich, 1923.

Döring, Detlef. *Pufendorf-Studien: Beiträge zur Biographie Samuel von Pufendorfs und zu seiner Entwicklung als Historiker und theologischer Schriftsteller.* Berlin: Duncker & Humblot, 1992.

————. "Säkularisierung und Moraltheologie bei Samuel von Pufendorf."
Zeitschrift für Theologie und Kirche 90 (1993): 156–74.

————. "Untersuchungen zur Entwicklung der theologischen und reli-
gionspolitischen Vorstellungen Samuel von Pufendorfs." In *Religion und
Religiosität im Zeitalter des Barock*, part 2, 873–82, ed. Dieter Breuer.
Wiesbaden: Harrassowitz, 1995.

————. "Samuel von Pufendorf and Toleration." In *Beyond the Persecuting
Society. Religious Toleration before the Enlightenment*, 178–96, ed. John C.
Laursen and Cary J. Nederman. Philadelphia: University of Pennsylvania
Press, 1998.

Dreitzel, Horst. "Gewissensfreiheit und soziale Ordnung. Religionstoleranz
als Problem der politischen Theorie am Ausgang des 17. Jahrhunderts."
Politische Vierteljahresschrift 36 (1995): 3–34.

————. "Toleranz und Gewissensfreiheit im konfessionellen Zeitalter. Zur
Diskussion im Reich zwischen Augsburger Religionsfrieden und Aufklä-
rung." In *Religion und Religiosität im Zeitalter des Barock*, part 1, 115–28,
ed. Dieter Breuer. Wiesbaden: Harrassowitz, 1995.

Hunter, Ian. "Religious Toleration and the Pluralisation of Personhood.
Christian Thomasius' Program for the Deconfessionalisation of Society."
Southern Review 31, no. 1 (1998): 38–53.

Lezius, Friedrich. *Der Toleranzbegriff Lockes und Pufendorfs. Ein Beitrag zur
Geschichte der Gewissensfreiheit*. Second reprint of the Leipzig 1900 edition. Aalen: Scientia, 1987.

Link, Christoph. *Herrschaftsordnung und bürgerliche Freiheit. Grenzen der
Staatsgewalt in der älteren deutschen Staatslehre*, 240–52. Vienna: Böhlau,
1979.

————. "Christentum und moderner Staat. Zur Grundlegung eines frei-
heitlichen Staatskirchentums im Aufklärungszeitalter." In *Christentum,
Säkularisation und modernes Recht*, 853–72, ed. L. L. Vallauri and
G. Dilcher. Milan: Giuffre, 1981.

Rabe, Horst. *Naturrecht und Kirche bei Samuel von Pufendorf*. Cologne:
Böhlau, 1958.

Stolleis, Michael. "Religion und Politik im Zeitalter des Barock. 'Konfes-
sionalisierung' oder 'Säkularisierung' bei der Entstehung des frühmo-
dernen Staates?" In *Religion und Religiosität im Zeitalter des Barock*, part
1, 23–42, ed. Dieter Breuer. Wiesbaden: Harrassowitz, 1995.

Zurbuchen, Simone. *Naturrecht und natürliche Religion. Zur Geschichte des*

Toleranzbegriffs von Samuel Pufendorf bis Jean-Jacques Rousseau. Würzburg: Königshausen & Neumann, 1991.

————. "Samuel Pufendorf's Concept of Toleration." In *Difference and Dissent: Theories of Toleration in Medieval and Early Modern Europe,* 163–84, ed. Cary J. Nederman and John C. Laursen. Lanham, Md.: Rowman & Littlefield, 1996.

————. "From Denominationalism to Enlightenment: Pufendorf, Le Clerc, and Thomasius on Toleration." In *Religious Toleration: "The Variety of Rites" from Cyrus to Defoe,* 191–209, ed. John C. Laursen. New York: St. Martin's, 1999.

INDEX

absolution, power of: God's authority for, 46–47; Kingdom of Heaven and, 44–46; sovereignty and, 42–43. *See also* forgiveness of sins.

accountability, in natural religion, 14–15

alms, 63, 67; power of church to collect, 89; in primitive church, 95. *See also* revenues

Apologia pro Christianis (Athenagoras), 87, 87 n. 187

apostasy, rejection of, 68

apostles: access to princes not sought, 91–92; commission from Christ, 37–39; enjoined from avarice, 54–56; gift of miracles to, 38, 54, 70; God's authority for absolution and, 46–47; Gospel published by, 88; having no power to command, 39–41; as missionaries, 36–37; moral precepts of, 40–41; power granted equally to, 50–51; power of excommunication, 51; power to constitute teachers, 88; power to plant churches, 87–88; preaching by, 36–37, 87; as stewards, 43; true church founded by, 118; unable to establish temporal sovereignty, 65; weapons of, 39–40

apostolic church, 118

Apostolic Creed, 117

arbitration, to decide controversies, 90

Article of Justification, 22–23

articles of faith: consultation on, 61; established by sovereign, 102–3; false, introduction of, 79–80; instruction of believers in, 72–73; inward consent to, 103. *See also* faith

assembly, church as, 59–60

Athenagoras, 35, 35 n. 51, 87, 87 n. 187

Augsburg Confession, 111

authority. *See* heavenly authority; sovereignty, temporal

avarice, apostles forbidden from, 54–56

bacchanals, 21, 21 n. 22

banishment, for heresy, 107–8

Bayle, Pierre, 40 n. 71

believers (Christians): consent of, in constitution of ministers, 97–98; free contributions to church, 95; instruction in articles of faith, 72–73; knowledge of mysteries of faith, 72; obligation to live unblemished life, 100; persecuted by popish clergy, 112; power to plant